# THINK LIKE A
# CADDIE
# PLAY LIKE A
# PRO

# THINK LIKE A
# CADDIE
# PLAY LIKE A
# PRO

### Golf's Top Caddies
### Reveal Their Winning
### Strategies

**James Y. Bartlett & the Professional Caddies Association**
Foreword by Arnold Palmer
Preface by Ben Crenshaw

SELLERS
PUBLISHING

## Published by Sellers Publishing, Inc.

Copyright © 2010 Tour Caddie Association, Inc. (dba) PCA Worldwide Inc.
All rights reserved.

Sellers Publishing, Inc.
161 John Roberts Road, South Portland, Maine 04106
For ordering information:
(800) 625-3386 toll free
Visit our Web site: www.sellerspublishing.com • E-mail: rsp@rsvp.com

ISBN: 13: 978-1-4162-0570-8
Library of Congress Control Number: 2009936729

No portion of this book may be reproduced or transmitted in any form,
or by any means, electronic or mechanical, including photographing, recording,
or by any information and storage retrieval system, without written permission
from the publisher.

10 9 8 7 6 5 4 3 2 1

Printed and bound in China.

# Contents

Foreword by Arnold Palmer     7

Preface by Ben Crenshaw     9

Introduction     11

## Chapter 1
### From Cadets to Caddies:
### A Short History of a Longstanding Tradition     17

## Chapter 2
### Tapping Into Your Inner Caddie     33

## Chapter 3
### The Game Plan: Charting *Your* Course for the Win     43

## Chapter 4
### Prep for Success: Why Warming Up Matters     59

## Chapter 5
### It's Element-ary!     73

## Chapter 6
### The Name of the Game Is Strategy     85

## Chapter 7
### Mastering the Greens     107

## Chapter 8
### Count 'Em Up: How the Stats Can Work for You     121

## Chapter 9
### Make Room for Caddie     133

## Chapter 10
### The Caddie Hall of Fame     143

Acknowledgments     158

About the Authors     159

Photo Credits     160

# Foreword

I've been blessed to have worked with several excellent caddies during my career. I've also had some bad ones, which helped me realize how invaluable a good man on the bag can be.

Of course, caddies don't make the shots — although a lot of them like to take credit for the good ones. As a competitor, I usually had a good idea of what I wanted to do on a hole or for a particular shot. But I always used my caddie for two things: information and confirmation. The caddie would give me the facts about a shot, which usually helped me confirm in my mind that my choice for the next shot was the right one.

Like any golfer, I made a few shots and missed a few as well but, having that base of information and the confidence that a good caddie instills, making the good shots was much easier.

Congratulations to the Professional Caddies Association for the work it does for kids, caddies, and the game. I hope that this book will help all golfers learn to gather the right kinds of information and rely on their inner caddie to make the best shot every time.

— *Arnold Palmer*

# Preface

One of the stories in this book is about how Carl Jackson, my caddie at Augusta National Golf Club, took a look at a couple of my practice swings, recommended two minor changes, and then helped me win the Masters in 1995. Carl was, as always, a steady and comforting influence on my game that week. A week when I especially needed his guidance and support, following the death of my friend and teacher, Harvey Penick.

That part of the player-caddie relationship is often overlooked. Sure, our caddies provide us with information about the yardage, the wind, and other important facts, but a really good caddie also serves as head cheerleader and helps keep a steady hand on the emotional tiller. In a golf tournament, especially a major one, emotions, stress, and tension run high, and a calm, humorous, and steady caddie is invaluable as we navigate our way around the golf course.

I often think about little Eddie Lowery, lugging around clubs almost bigger than he was, for Francis Ouimet at the 1913 U.S. Open at Brookline. It surely made Francis smile to watch his ten-year-old buddy, walking like a bantam rooster down those hallowed fairways, as the pair improbably vanquished the British giants of the day, Vardon and Ray. Once Eddie got his hands on that bag, he was not letting it go, and that must have helped Ouimet's confidence and resolve that famous weekend.

I've been blessed to work with some really good caddies in my career, especially Emil Smith, Jeff Burrell, Tony Navarro, Linn Strickler, Carl Jackson, Bobbie Millen, and James Haugh. I think the critical characteristics that these caddies had in common — their cool and calm demeanors, great concentration, and utter confidence in themselves — are things that a weekend golfer can learn from. Golf is a game with many ups and downs; but the golfer who can approach it with a positive attitude and an upbeat approach will usually get much better results.

For the golfer who wants to improve his game, and especially win more, thinking like a caddie is a good first step. I congratulate the PCA for all the great contributions to golf that they make.

*— Ben Crenshaw*

# Introduction

Jack Nicklaus always said that the most important six inches in golf are those that lie between the left ear and the right. This book was written to help each golfer put those six inches to work.

This is not intended to be a book that will help you with golf instruction or swing mechanics. There are plenty of other titles on the bookshelf or in the DVD bin that can do that. Rather, this book is intended to provide golfers with insight into competitive preparation and play, course strategies, and clear thinking on the golf course. In other words, *this is a book about how to win on the golf course*. Every golfer or person interested in the game will benefit from the inside tips and advice provided by the world's top caddies in this book.

Due largely to the rise in popularity of the golf cart or buggy in the mid-twentieth century, many golfers today have never had the experience of playing a round of golf with a caddie. Yet every professional touring golfer depends on the caddie to not only carry the clubs, keep them clean, and provide an accurate yardage for each shot, but to serve as a valuable team member in the ongoing effort to shoot the lowest possible score.

**Think Like a Caddie, Play Like a Pro** will draw on the combined experience of some of the best and most famous caddies of past and present days to reveal a totally new perspective on the royal and ancient game of golf. This entertaining and useful guide will show golfers of every level the most important aspects of the game, including:

- how to prepare for a round

- how to plan and strategize for lower scores

- how to avoid trouble and get out of it

- how to stay mentally alert

- how to use the rules for one's benefit

- and dozens of other score-reducing secrets

Jack Nicklaus, the Golden Bear, lining up a putt with the help of his caddie and son, Steve.

This book will encourage every golfer to connect with his "inner caddie" in thinking about how to play the game, how to manage one's way around a course, and how to deal with all the situations that come up during a round of golf, whether it's a friendly weekend Nassau, or a club championship.

Sports psychologists make thousands of dollars trying to train their clients to ignore and eliminate these distracting inner voices that divert attention and are such a hindrance to good performance on the golf course. "Stay in the moment," they tell us. "Think only about the shot in front of you right now."

The shrinks are right, of course. Concentration and good performance are inextricably linked. Inner talk is confusing, destructive, self-defeating and, alas, almost impossible to control.

Touring professionals are good at staying in the moment and focusing only on the job at hand — hitting the golf ball to the target they want. But they also have a not-so-secret weapon that most of us do not: the caddie. Almost every caddie interviewed in the preparation of this book claimed that the single most important job they have is to keep their player confident and positive. Caddies never speak in negative terms and do not allow their player to speak that way either. Caddie talk — which is always out loud, as opposed to our "inner" talk — is all about the shot at hand, not the last one or the next one. The caddie brings his player into the here and now, where the task is to hit the golf ball to an exact and specific location, whether that is on a distant fairway, a nearby green, or into the awaiting cup. The caddie offers information and advice that is directed only to that one task: hit this ball to that spot. Nothing else matters.

Let's imagine a golfer named John playing without a caddie in a typical weekend Nassau with his friends. We'll join his thoughts in progress as he approaches an important shot in the match:

> OK, there's the 150-yard marker. Hundred fifty. 7-iron. Pin looks like it's back some, so I'd better hit this hard. Three holes ago, I pushed my 7 to the right, so this time I'll aim left just in case that happens again. Of course, there's that deep bunker on the left. Don't want to go in there! Took me three swings to get out of that bunker last week! Killed my score. Awful! I always suck in the sand. Hmm, I think I hit my 7 last week, too. Pulled it! OK, I'll aim right so that doesn't happen again. I've got to keep my head down. Hit it hard. Don't pull it. Don't push it. Gotta get this on

the green or we'll be four down. Damn that Charlie . . . he's made every putt he's looked at today! I can't believe it . . . he usually 3-putts. OK . . . how's the position of my feet? Pointing the right way? This stance doesn't feel quite right . . . I'll move 'em a little to the right. OK, that's good. Ready? Go!

We won't describe what happens to John's approach shot. You can probably imagine.

Now, let's put Joe the Pro in the same situation, only he has his trusty caddie Woody by his side. Let's listen in to their discussion:

> **JOE PRO:** Man, did you see the Celtics last night? They were rockin'! OK, what do we have?
>
> **WOODY:** You've got 137 to the front, plus 18 to the pin. That's 155. There's some room behind, so we're good to go for it
>
> **JOE PRO:** Wind feels like it's against us a bit.
>
> **WOODY:** Yup. It's in our face and coming in about eleven o'clock.
>
> **JOE PRO:** I'm thinking 6.
>
> **WOODY:** I like that play. You don't have to kill it. You've got room behind. I'd start it at that pine tree and let the wind carry it back in.
>
> **JOE PRO:** OK.
>
> **WOODY:** Nice and smooth. Plenty of room.  Piece of cake.

See the difference? Our amateur John's mind is racing a mile a minute, filling his head with scenarios of failure. Other than a very rough yardage, he has not spent a nanosecond thinking about his shot. Thanks to his hyperactive inner voice, he's fidgeting and nervous, uncommitted, uncertain, and worried about things that don't really matter. The result? He's on his way to making a bad shot.

Joe Pro, on the other hand, has gone from talking about the Celtics to zeroing in on the task at hand. His caddie Woody gives him the numbers he needs, reconfirms the wind speed and direction, points out the space behind the pin, gives him an aiming point, and, finally, plants some thoughts that will build Joe's confidence: Nice and smooth. Plenty of room. Piece of cake.

The purpose of this book is to show you how professional caddies work, strategize, and perform on the golf course so you — the player — can begin to think the same way. If you can begin to think like a caddie in your approach to the game, you will find yourself beginning to play a better round of golf.

The above scenario of how a golfer and his caddie begin to focus in on the strategy and purpose of every shot is just one example of how you can begin to retrain yourself to think like a caddie to play like a pro. Instead of feeling like a victim of circumstances, the player collaborates with his caddie and together — operating as a team — they approach each new shot as a fresh opportunity, a clean slate. There is a plan for every hole and every shot.

And that's where those important cranial six inches come into play: all it takes is making yourself stop and think like a caddie would. Make your mind analyze the situation at hand. Go through a mental checklist just as you go through a pre-shot routine. Eliminate all thoughts that have nothing to do with the task at hand, figure out the easiest and least risky shot you can make, depending on conditions and circumstances, and then execute your plan.

It sounds easy. That's because it is. When you think like a caddie, there is nothing left to chance or happenstance. You warm up with a purpose, play the round one shot at a time, analyze the results with cool detachment after the round, and make adjustments to the strategy for the next round. You approach the game with quiet confidence as well as a sense of fun, and play with greater pleasure.

Most golfers find it liberating to engage in this kind of teamwork: to listen as the caddie provides important data for each shot and offers words of encouragement, making the game easier and a lot more fun.  Indeed, when a caddie hands you a 7-iron, tells you to aim it at that tree or this mound and let it fly, you'll want to follow his lead. "Hey," you'll think to yourself, "he just told me exactly what I need to know to make the shot. I can do that!"

But how can a golfer who plays without a caddie get the same benefits?  Only by shifting gears and starting to think like a caddie. In our example above, John would achieve much better results if he developed a plan for each shot, gathering the data he needs before actually making the shot, and focusing his attention only on the task at hand, and not on the results either before or after.

In other words, if John learns to think like a caddie, he'll have a much better chance of playing like a pro.

In the pages of this book, you will hear the voices of professional caddies — both those who work on the pro tours and those who work day in and day out at some of the finer private country clubs looping for ordinary golfers. They will share their secrets on how they get the best out of their players. These insider tips and words of advice can be utilized by any golfer to develop a strategic and intelligent attitude towards golf that will result in a less stressful game and lower scores.  As you go for your shot, you'll begin to size up the situation more astutely and confidently.  The distracting inner chatter will be replaced by more a positive message: *Nice and smooth. Plenty of room. Piece of cake.*

The late Payne Stewart gets some information on the wind from caddie Mike Hicks.

Of course, you the golfer still have to hit the shots, and we all know that even the pros miss shots on occasion. But when you begin to think like a caddie — developing a plan, sticking to it, approaching each shot with confidence — you'll find that you'll make better choices, avoid getting into trouble and, as a result, begin to play within your own abilities, utilizing your strengths, minimizing your weaknesses, and scoring better than you thought possible.

So get those six inches between your ears engaged and ready. This book will help you think clearer, play smarter, and win more often.  All you have to do is think like a caddie!

# Chapter 1

## From Cadets to Caddies

"A good caddie is more than a mere assistant.
He is a guide, philosopher, and friend."

— *Henry Longhurst*

# 1

# From Cadets to Caddies:
## A Short History of a Longstanding Tradition

When Ben Crenshaw arrived at the Augusta National Golf Club for the Masters tournament in the spring of 1995, winning was probably one of the last things on his mind. Although he had won his first Green Jacket in 1984 and knew and loved the course at Augusta, his game was in disarray — he'd missed the cut in three of his last four tournaments and he hadn't shot a round in the 60s for several months. And no sooner had he arrived in Augusta than he received word that his beloved mentor and longtime teacher, Harvey Penick, had died back in Austin, Texas. Heartbroken, Crenshaw flew home on Tuesday of Masters week to serve as a pallbearer at Penick's funeral.

When he came back to Augusta, Crenshaw finally turned to his game. He and his favorite caddie at Augusta National, Carl Jackson, headed out to the practice range alongside Magnolia Drive. Crenshaw began hitting balls under Jackson's experienced and watchful eyes. After a couple of minutes, Jackson spoke a few quiet words to his man: "Put the ball a little bit back in your stance, Ben. And you got to turn your shoulders more."

One for the ages: Ben Crenshaw collapses into Carl Jackson's arms after winning the 1995 Masters.

The next four balls Crenshaw hit were dead-solid perfect. It was like a light had finally snapped on again. "I've never had a confidence transformation like that in my life," Crenshaw said later. Over the next four days, Crenshaw rode his caddie's tip and a wave of emotion to shoot 70-67-69-68 to capture his second Masters title by a single stroke over Davis Love III. After he holed out on the 72nd green, Gentle Ben bent from the waist, held his head in his hands, and cried, overcome by all the emotion of the week. Carl Jackson reached over and held him in his arms, an enduring image of the relationship that can develop between a golfer and his caddie.

In 1913, when a tall, gangly twenty-year-old caddie at The Country Club near Boston qualified for the U.S. Open championship at the course across the street from his own home, no one expected him to last against the best field of American professionals (many of whom were Scottish-born) as well as the overwhelming favorites from Britain: Harry Vardon and Ted Ray. Indeed, by the time Francis Ouimet got ready to tee off, all the top caddies at the club had been snapped up by the other competitors. At the last moment, Francis agreed to let his persistent neighborhood friend, Eddie Lowery, carry his clubs. The picture of the ten-year-old Lowery struggling with a golf bag almost bigger than he was is a priceless memory of that weekend. When, after the first three rounds, Ouimet was tied for the lead with Vardon and Ray, officials tried to get him to fire little Eddie and get a "real" caddie, but he refused: Lowery's unfailing belief in Francis and his underdog attitude served as a good luck charm for Ouimet. And the luck held: after sinking two dramatic putts on the last two holes, the three golfers remained tied, and in the 18-hole playoff the next day, Francis Ouimet won handily. The stunning upset was national news and both Francis Ouimet and little Eddie Lowery became instant celebrities.

Many, if not most, of the brightest golf names from the golden era of golf, in the years between the wars, got their start in the game as caddies. It was by carrying clubs, watching other golfers, and absorbing the fine points of the game that golfers like Sam Snead, Ben Hogan, Byron Nelson, and Gene Sarazen (to name just a few) picked up the strategies and techniques that served them well once they became professional golfers. Countless others, including captains of industry, learned the tenets of the game and its unique system of etiquette and sportsmanship by working as caddies in their younger years.

The winning team: Francis Ouimet (right) and his 10-year-old caddie Eddie Lowery on their way to winning the 1913 U.S. Open at Brookline, Massachusetts.

## Helping Ben Carry the Weight

Caddie Carl Jackson recently talked about that week in April 1995, recalling how Ben Crenshaw was preparing for the Masters at Augusta National (see Page 15) when he learned on Sunday before the tournament that his longtime friend and mentor, Harvey Penick, had passed away.

On Monday, Crenshaw played a practice round in preparation for the tournament. Jackson recalled that Crenshaw was "a bit lost" with his golf swing. "He was out of position with his swing and he had poor ball position," Jackson said. As Crenshaw prepared to tee off on the ninth hole, Jackson headed down the fairway with his bag to wait for him. "I looked back at the tee and I could see that Ben was really reaching for the ball," Jackson said. "I said to myself, 'Dang, Ben, you look like you're playing hockey back there.' That's when I realized he was out of position, which was causing his bad shots."

When Crenshaw walked down the fairway to where Jackson was waiting, the caddie told him what he had observed and suggested they head for the practice range. "Once we got to the range, he hit a few balls and he knew immediately that he had found something he could work with," Jackson said. "I remember sitting down on the ground just a few inches from the ball to show him he was out of position and coming over the top. He got his swing wound tight and improved his tempo and started striking the ball really good from that point on."

On Tuesday evening, Crenshaw flew from Georgia to Texas where he was a pallbearer at his teacher's funeral the next day. "At the funeral, Ben told his brother that he was excited and felt like we had come up with something that was really good for his game," Jackson said. Sure enough, when Crenshaw returned to Augusta, despite a heavy heart, he played with confidence and, as his mentor had long preached, he "took dead aim" at his second green jacket. "Knowing Ben, and guessing how the spectators would be giving him condolences during the round, I took it upon myself to get him refocused on the shot at hand," Jackson said. "Ben was carrying a lot of weight and I was helping him carry it."

The picture (see page 18) of the emotionally spent golfer and his caddie on the 18th green, after the final putt dropped, shows how heavy that weight had been.

— *Mark Nelson*

Ben Crenshaw and his caddie, Carl Jackson, walk up the first fairway during the first round of the Masters at the Augusta National Golf Club.

Sadly, this way of introducing new generations of golfers to the game almost disappeared from the scene following the Second World War, when the golf cart, and the revenue-generating bonanza it represented, became popular in the United States. Merle Williams of Long Beach, California, first devised a battery-operated car for his wife's shopping runs during the gas-rationing days of wartime. After the war, he started making electric vehicles for industrial use, and then, in 1952 he created the first golf cart. By 1960, his Marketeer Company was the largest supplier of golf carts to the industry. The immense enthusiasm for riding in a cart while playing golf, a uniquely American habit, swept the game and ended the long tradition of the caddie at many country clubs and golf courses.

Only in the last decade, as there's been a movement to return more exercise to the game, has walking a course and playing with a caddie gained renewed popularity with some golfers. This, in turn, has led to the beginning of a resurgence in caddie programs around the country. But the replacement of local caddies by carts meant professional golfers on the pro tours had to look harder for competent help. At the same time, the prize money being offered on the tours meant that the entire game had to become more professional – and serious. Professional golfers began to practice more, work out more, and to devise new ways to raise the level of their games. Instead of just depending on a local fellow to cart the clubs around the course, pro golfers started to demand much more from their caddies, which led to today's era of specialization.

## "A WIFE WITHOUT 'BENEFITS'"

The caddie has been part of the game of golf since its beginnings. But the role of the caddie as a vital contributor to a player's success on the professional tour is of relatively recent historical vintage. Until the middle of the twentieth century, when motorized golf carts replaced human caddies throughout the United States, even professional golfers rarely employed full-time caddies, relying instead on a ready supply of local lads at each tour stop. In the era when every country club had a caddie yard and an abundance of teenagers willing to lug members' bags around for fifty cents a loop, the touring pros could count on finding a caddie who knew the golf course, could add up the yardages, and would keep the clubs clean after each shot.

"The player may experiment about his swing, his grip, his stance. It is only when he begins asking his caddie's advice that he is getting on dangerous ground."
—Sir W.G. Simpson, author of
*The Art of Golf*, published in 1887

But the modern era of golf is radically different in so many ways, not least of which is the size of the purses at stake. Technology and specialization have changed the royal and ancient game, and the modern-day role of the caddie has changed as well. In the high-pressure world of today's professional game, the caddie has been elevated to the position of co-competitor, someone the player depends on, not just to have the clubs and yardages ready, but to serve as coach, sports psychologist, swing guru, strategist, navigator, security chief, workout buddy, and boon companion. It is, said one caddie who wished not to be identified, "like being a wife, without 'benefits!'"

While many of these modern-day duties are somewhat new to the role of the caddie, they are not far different from the role first envisioned three centuries ago when the rules were initially encoded by the Honourable Company of Edinburgh Golfers at the Links of Leith in 1744. From the beginning of the game, the caddie has been considered part of 'the side' in any golf competition, an equal member of the team along with the one who actually makes the shots. The caddie is recognized in the rules as the only one who can legally provide advice to the golfer during a competitive round. Likewise, if a caddie commits a breach of the rules, his player suffers the penalty.

## HOW IT ALL BEGAN

Caddies show up in some of the earliest historical references to the game. In 1628, the household accounts of the Marquess of Montrose, one of the great Scottish clan chiefs, described a payment to a caddie who was "the boy who carried my Lord's clubs to the field." Sir John Foulis of Ravelston is recorded as paying the sum of four shillings to "the boy who carried my clubs" in 1672.

The very name "caddie" is considered a Scottish derivation of the French word cadet, which was originally used to describe the not-first-born sons of the French aristocrats who accompanied Mary Stuart, Queen of Scots, to Edinburgh when she assumed the Scottish crown in 1542. In its original French meaning, the word translated as "young son" or "young chief," and since those sons who would not inherit a noble title often joined the military, the word came to mean a young officer-in-training, as in the cadets of West Point. By the eighteenth century, however, a Scotsman would understand the word cadet, which he pronounced and spelled "caddie," to mean a porter, errand-runner, or general helper to an important personage. And since most important personages in Scotland played the game of golf, the meaning gradually shifted to define the person who carried the clubs for his gentleman employer.

Many players in those early days would simply employ a caddie to carry their golfing sticks (golf bags only came into use in the 1880s) and keep an eye on errant shots. The caddie's other main job was to tee the ball, which meant creating a small hill of sand or mud upon which the ball was placed, usually right on the putting green adjacent to the hole just completed — it wasn't until the mid-nineteenth century that separate teeing grounds became commonplace. Keeping track of the clubs was a bit of a challenge in the age of the featherie and the gutta-percha balls, as golfers utilized an often-bewildering variety of clubs (the modern fourteen-club limit did not come into effect until 1939).

Still, even some early golfers understood that having an experienced and knowledgeable caddie often resulted in winning the game. In 1682, the Duke of York (the Stuart who became King James II of England and James VII of Scotland) was challenged to a golfing match at Leith Links by two English noblemen who claimed that English golf was superior to that of Scotland. The Duke was allowed to choose his own partner for the match, and he named a common shoemaker named John Paterstone (who turned out to be something of a ringer!). At the Duke's side for the match was his trusted caddie, Andrew Dickson. The Scottish side won the match. Dickson was obviously knowledgeable in golf, as he went on to a successful career as a club maker.

History also records the caddies favored by two upper-crust champions who played their golf in St. Andrews. Captain Maitland Dougall, an early nineteenth-century champion, was never seen on the course without his man, Sandy Pirie, at his side. Later in that century, Sandy Herd was the caddie of choice for Sir John Whyte-Melville, who kept him busy: the gentleman was known for playing thirty-six holes three days a week, year-round, no matter the weather. Both these

> "Friends noticed that the caddie always walked barefoot. It was his duty when [Errol] Flynn's ball went in the rough, to pick it up with his unusually long toes and, without stooping down, deposit it quietly on the fairway."
>
> —*The New Yorker* (1937)

Steve Williams and Tiger Woods have helped redefine the caddie's roles in today's world of championship golf.

gentlemen obviously appreciated the value of having a caddie who knew not only every inch of the Old Course, but every quirk and flaw of their own swings as well.

Like Andrew Dickson, many early caddies had more than one role in the game. Davie Robertson of St. Andrews was renowned as a great instructor of the game, and also played in some of the earliest professional matches of his era. But his main occupation was as caddie at the Old Course. His son, Allan Robertson, was named Keeper of the Links (similar to today's golf professional) and also made golf clubs and balls.

When the game of golf migrated across the Atlantic to the United States, caddies came along. As American golf began to grow in the late nineteenth century and the early years of the twentieth century, a large number of Scotsmen emigrated to take up jobs as teachers, instructors, and caddie-masters at the new country clubs springing up around the country.

## A NEW ERA FOR CADDIES

One of the first famous players to hire a full-time caddie to travel with him and work at every event was Jack Nicklaus, whose caddie was Angelo Argea. With his bushy, gray-white Afro and Fu Manchu mustache, Angelo was almost as instantly recognizable as the Golden Bear himself. The two first began working together in 1963 at the Palm Springs Classic, and for the next twenty years, Argea was on the bag for some forty-four of Nicklaus's seventy-three PGA Tour victories and later went on to market his own brand of yardage books for resorts.

Soon, most of the big-name pros were doing the same as Jack. There have been other famous pairings through the years: Gary Player and Rabbit Dyer, Lee Trevino and Herman Mitchell, Ben Crenshaw and Carl Jackson, Tom Watson and Bruce Edwards, Phil Mickelson and Bones Mackay, and Nick Faldo and Fanny Sunesson. And, of course, there is today's most famous pair: Tiger Woods and Steve Williams.

When Woods first came out on the PGA Tour in 1996, his advisors felt he needed an experienced caddie to help guide him around the tour's courses, so they hired Mike "Fluff" Cowan, the longtime caddie for Peter Jacobsen. Two years later, Team Tiger replaced Fluff with New Zealand native Steve Williams, who had been caddying on the PGA Tour since he was sixteen for the likes of Greg Norman and Raymond Floyd. In addition to his professional skills, Williams was younger than Cowan and shared Tiger's mania for physical fitness. The partnership, so far, has been one of the most successful in the history of the game and has helped make Williams, forty-six, one of the richest sportsmen in his native New Zealand.

The history of golfer-caddie relationships is replete with touching examples that illustrate how strong the bond between a player and a caddie can be. Jeff "Squeaky" Medlin was a veteran caddie of considerable skill who worked for South African pro Nick Price. But at the 1991 PGA Championship at Crooked Stick in Indiana, Medlin found himself with an unlikely employer after Price had to withdraw from the tournament. John Daly, a raw-boned bomber from Arkansas with a long backswing and blonde mullet, got into the tournament as the ninth alternate. Medlin hooked on with Daly for the week and helped him make history. After an opening round 69, Daly, who had not even played a practice round, followed up with scores of 67-69-71 and won the championship by three strokes over Bruce Lietzke. "Squeaky" Medlin, who derived his nickname from his high-pitched voice, spurred his man to victory by handing Daly his driver on each tee and imploring, "Kill!" Daly credited Medlin with keeping him focused and energized en route to the most surprising victory in the history of the championship.

Bruce Edwards started caddying for Tom Watson in 1973 and, except for two years when he worked for Greg Norman, stayed with him until 2003. Over the course of their thirty years together, Watson and Edwards developed a relationship that transcended their time together on the golf course. Edwards was on the bag for many of Watson's victories. In 2003, Edwards was diagnosed with ALS, amyotrophic lateral sclerosis (commonly known as Lou Gehrig's disease) but continued to work for Watson until he was physically unable to make it around the course.

Perhaps the most touching moment that underscored their relationship took place during the 2003 U.S. Open, when spectators at Olympia Fields greeted Edwards with cries of "Bruuuuucce, Bruuuuucce!" as he and Watson made their way up the 18th fairway on the way to a 65 that put Watson in contention for the tournament lead. "Knowing Tom," said Edwards, his speech slurred (one of the effects of ALS), on NBC Sports, "he did it for me." When Edwards succumbed to his disease the following April, Watson spearheaded fundraising for ALS research, donating a $1 million annuity that came with his victory in the Charles Schwab Cup. "He's not with us in body, but he's with us in spirit," Watson said after Edwards died. "I'm relying on his spirit to take care of me." Ben Crenshaw, who had selected Edwards to be in charge of the caddies at the 1999 Ryder Cup, said, "It's not a good day for any of us. He was a real professional and one of the most positive human beings I've ever been around. It's not fair. They took a good one there."

These and other modern-day examples are indicative of the way the touring pro has come to depend on his caddie for far more than a good yardage or the read of a putt. Today's caddies are integral parts of the team that each golfer

Tom Watson and his longtime caddie Bruce Edwards, who tragically died of ALS (Lou Gehrig's disease).

brings to a tournament every week, including the agent, sports psychologist, swing guru, and physical therapist. While the basic duties of the caddie haven't changed in hundreds of years, the role they play has expanded and become increasingly more important. As Henry Longhurst, the great British golf writer and broadcaster, once said, "A good caddie is more than a mere assistant. He is guide, philosopher, and friend."

It is that role of the caddie as co-competitor, strategist, second pair of eyes, helpmate, and guide that is so crucial to success and to scoring in today's game. And it is that aspect of the caddie's role that is the focus of this book.

In their heyday, Jack Nicklaus (right) and caddie Angelo Argea were a famous pairing.

# Caddie Highs and Lows

- **Andrew Dickson**

  The first caddie in recorded history, he caddied for the Duke of York (later King James II) in 1681 and 1682. He was on the Duke's bag when, to settle a bet about which nation invented golf, the Duke and a local Edinburgh shoemaker named John Paterstone drummed a pair of English noblemen at Leith Links.

- **Eddie Lowery**

  Just ten years old and barely bigger than the clubs he carried, Eddie looped for his neighborhood chum, the twenty-year-old Francis Ouimet, when he won the U.S. Open in 1913 at The Country Club, stunning the world.

- **Angelo Argea**

  His permed hair and Fu Manchu mustache made him easily as recognizable as his man, the great Jack Nicklaus, during the 1960s and '70s. Jack fired Angelo when he failed to measure off yardages one week — Angelo went into business publishing yardage guides.

- **Carl "Skillet" Jackson**

  In 1983, the Masters changed its rules to allow players to import their own regular caddies, rather than use the club's own caddie corps. One player who refused was Ben Crenshaw, who stayed loyal to his local man. Jackson rewarded the Texan by helping him win two Green Jackets, the first in 1984 and the last in 1995.

- **Mike "Fluff" Cowan**

  Longtime caddie for Peter Jacobsen, Fluff was chosen by Tiger Woods to become part of his entourage when Tiger first went on tour. After almost three successful years, Tiger and Fluff parted ways and created an opening for Steve Williams to get on his bag.

- **Christophe (last name never given, "for tax purposes")**

  Frenchman Jean Van de Velde's silent partner on the last hole of the 1999 British Open watched as Van de Velde, holding a three-shot lead, made risky shot after risky shot on his way to a triple-bogey 7 on the hole. All agreed in hindsight that Christophe should have made his man play the hole more conservatively, since even a double-bogey would have led Van de Velde to a win.

- **Miles Byrne**

  In contention entering the final round of the 2001 British Open at Royal Lytham & St. Anne's, Ian Woosnam birdied the first hole. Then his caddie informed him that he had forgotten to remove from the bag an extra driver Woosnam had been trying out on the practice range. The two-stroke penalty spelled the end of Woosie's chances. He kept Byrne on his bag, but a few weeks later, Miles was late for a round and got the sack.

# Chapter 2
## Tapping Into Your Inner Caddie

"Top caddies always think, 'What's happening next?
What's the next hole? How's that hole playing? Which way is
the wind blowing there? Can we fire at the hole?'"

— *Steve Williams,*
*caddie for Tiger Woods*

Caddie Steve Williams giving Tiger Woods his input on making a challenging shot.

# 2

# Tapping Into Your Inner Caddie

## THE CONFIDENCE GAME

Playing golf with confidence can be one of the hardest things to do. The game is always attacking our sense of self-assurance, if not our very psyches, and approaching even a straightforward golf shot with the sense that this might be a simple thing to do is never easy.

Professional caddies know that getting their player into the right frame of mind is the most important thing they do.

> *Making sure my player is confident before playing a shot is 100 percent important. There's no point in a player standing over a shot if they're not confident. Those are the things you've got to look for. If you sense he's not confident you have to talk to him, call him off the shot, talk about it and give him the confidence to do it. Likewise, when a guy is going along, swinging well, playing with confidence, you can take more aggressive lines. And you can talk about that confidence: "Hey, you're swinging good."*
>
> —Steve Williams, caddie for Tiger Woods

## How Larry, Moe, and Curly Helped My Swing

The single best lesson I ever had in the game of golf came from a caddie. I was traveling through Ireland, and somewhere between Killarney and Cork I completely mislaid whatever semblance of a golf swing I once possessed. Hey, it happens.

In any case, on the 1st tee at Mount Juliet near Kilkenny, I apologized in advance to the stout middle-aged man, bundled in a dirty blue parka, who had the misfortune to be huddling next to my golf bag. "You drew the wrong straw today, my good man," I told him, and proceeded to demonstrate on the 1st hole. Weak drive, chunked approach, scalded bunker shot, weak return chip, two wobbly putts: easy double bogey. My sigh of self-disgust came from one of my deepest chakras.

Walking after my tee ball on the 2nd, my caddie spoke up. "What's funny to you, Jim?" he asked, clubs jingling as his stubby legs tried to keep up.

"Huh?"

"What makes you laugh?" he continued. "Some cartoon? Movie?"

I thought about his question for a minute, and, almost unbidden, The Three Stooges came to mind. Embarrassed, I confessed to my addiction, since childhood, to Larry, Moe, and Curly.

"Good!" he said, chuckling. "From now on, just t'ink of the Three Stooges before ye swing."

Amused, I tried out his advice. Before making the next swing, I envisioned Curly's "nyuk, nyuk, nyuk." Nailed a 5-iron to about fifteen feet. Looking over the putt, I heard in my mind "Wooo, wooo, wooo." It rimmed out. The next hole was a par 3. Moe slapped Larry, whose head made that coconut sound against Curly's, and I feathered one in over the pond to about ten feet. The kid was back. *Nyuk, nyuk, nyuk.*

— *James Y. Bartlett*

· · · · · · · · · · · · · · · · · · · · · · · · · · · · · · · · · · · · · ·

*It's not always the case that your player is 100 percent confident, but that's what most caddies aim for . . . to have the player's complete confidence, even if it ends up being wrong. We talk all the way through each shot. I give her the facts and then I can always tell if she's happy or unhappy with my suggestions. Ultimately, I have to make her realize that what she's about to do is absolutely 100 percent correct. Even if there's a little bit of doubt in my mind, I have to make her believe it's absolutely right. She can't go into a shot thinking, "This maybe isn't right." I'd rather a player put a good swing on it and be slightly wrong than put a bad swing on when it could be right.*
—Mike Patterson, caddie for Karie Webb

How can you get yourself into that confident state of mind, if you don't have a caddie cheerleader to cheer you on? Caddies and their players follow some very simple rules.

### RULE ONE: CHOOSE A SHOT YOU KNOW YOU CAN MAKE

During tournament play, professional golfers will never try a shot they've never made before, or one for which they know the percentages of success are low. The only exceptions to this rule come on the final few holes of a tournament when they have a chance to win or need a miracle.

But in the normal course of play, the player and his caddie will always select the easiest, most risk-free, and simplest shot demanded by the situation. The caddie will know how well his player is swinging that day and will lobby for the shot that will keep him out of trouble. Likewise, if he knows his player is on his game, the caddie will recommend a slightly more difficult line or provide an aiming point that has a bit more risk to it.

Can we cut off some of the corner of a dogleg from the tee? Challenge the deep bunker that lies to the left of the green? Try an approach shot to a pin placement on a narrow part of the green, with all kinds of lurking trouble? If the player is on his game, the answer might be yes. Golf is a constant battle between risk and reward, but for amateur players risk usually only leads to trouble and more strokes.

Therefore, the first thought your inner caddie should have in evaluating a shot should be "What is the safe play here?" rather than "Let's go for broke!"

Nick Faldo lines up a putt with the help of his caddie, Fanny Sunesson.

This can be difficult for many of us. Every golfer's instinct is to try the heroic shot, to get out of trouble by trying for the miraculous recovery, even though all of us know, deep down inside, that the successful, miraculous golf shot is as rare as a Tiger Woods double-bogey.

Let's say you've hit a poor drive on a long par 4, and you're facing a 225-yard shot to a green tightly guarded by bunkers and water. Your instinct is to make up for the poor shot by trying a hybrid club or a fairway metalwood to get the ball onto the green. It's a par 4, after all, and you're supposed to be on in 2.

Your inner caddie will say something like: "No, that's not a good idea. The lie in the rough isn't a good one, you don't have a good record with long, hybrid iron shots, there is a ton of trouble up there near the green, and if this shot doesn't come off, we're looking at a 6 or 7 at best. Let's take an 8-iron, make a nice easy swing, and just get the ball back in play and up near the green and we'll take our chances on making an up-and-down par. Even if that doesn't happen, we should make no worse than a bogey here."

Think about it. Your chances of making the long shot out of the rough to the green are long. However, your chances of hitting an 8-iron relatively straight to a spot in the fairway up near the green are excellent. Your inner caddie is telling you to play the percentages.

Every shot should be played with total confidence in its outcome. That means not attempting to do something you can't do, or have little chance of pulling off. It means evaluating the circumstances (lie, distance, weather conditions, wind) and choosing the shot you *know* you can make.

## RULE TWO: THINK ABOUT THE CONDITIONS THAT WILL IMPACT YOUR SHOT

> *Top caddies always think, "What's happening next? What's the next hole? How's that hole playing? Which way is the wind blowing there? Can we fire at the hole?"*
>
> *They're always thinking, "How's my player? How's he swinging today? How's he gonna play this hole today? What sort of shot is he gonna hit?"*
>
> *The caddie is always thinking. You're not just out there carrying the clubs and giving the yardage. I think the guys that are good caddies are always thinking ahead.*
>
> —Steve Williams, caddie for Tiger Woods

The average golfer is always thinking, too . . . but it's usually negative, or at least not helpful, thoughts that course through his head. Thoughts about the last bad shot he hit . . . about the putt he yanked two holes ago . . . how if he bogies this hole, he might shoot his highest round of the year.

The fine art of thinking like a caddie on the golf course involves recalibrating one's thought patterns into a more positive vein. Tiger's caddie, Steve Williams, is always thinking, but his thoughts are completely and totally focused on the task at hand and the shots that must be made. He is alert to the conditions surrounding him at any moment, checking the wind, the pin placements, the attitude of his player, maybe even the scores of those ahead of his player, so he can make informed judgments about the kinds of shots that will be needed.

Zen masters know that thoughts leap unbidden into the mind. The art of meditation that they teach consists of concentrating on nothing but one's own deep breathing, and requires the practitioner to consistently but firmly return one's thoughts to that simple in-and-out pattern as the mind begins to drift. And the mind *will* always drift or fill with internal chatter, idle thoughts, and strange tangents. Recall the scene at the end of *Ghostbusters* when the evil spirit compels the three heroes to choose their opponent and Dan Aykroyd's character tells them to empty their minds and think of nothing so they won't have to battle anyone. And, of course, Bill Murray's character immediately conjures up the Stay Puft Marshmallow Man, whom he envisions marching across Manhattan.

In the same vein, most players find it difficult to concentrate to the point where everything else is completely shut out. There are exceptions; one is Ben Hogan, who was paired one year at the Masters with Claude Harmon. On the famous par-3 12th hole, Ben hit a lovely shot onto the green and then Harmon stepped up and hit a better shot that rolled into the cup for an ace! The crowd went wild, of course, while Harmon walked up to the green and plucked the ball out of the hole. Hogan then drained his birdie putt to more sustained applause. On the next tee, Hogan said to Harmon, "You know, that's the first time I've ever birdied that hole! What did you have?"

But for those of us who are less than superhuman, it is impossible not to have our minds drifting while we play a round of golf. We talk with our playing partners, enjoy gossip and conversation, watch the groups in front of us taking their shots, and generally experience the game's ebb and flow around us.

But if one is channeling his inner caddie, he makes it a point to think, consciously and deliberately, about the conditions that will affect his next shot, and perhaps a few shots after that. All sports are

"Here's the thing . . . when a golfer gets in trouble, say in the deep rough . . . behind some trees or a bad lie in the bunker, and tries a miraculous recovery shot, I can almost guarantee he can't make the shot. He's never tried it before! But if he takes his medicine and gets back on the fairway, or at least in play, I can totally guarantee he'll have a next shot. And that's all the game is about, the next shot."
—Vince, longtime caddie at Aronimink GC Newtown Square, PA

activities that require a player's reaction, but unlike most other sports, in golf the player is not reacting to the motion of the ball, which is just sitting there, but rather *to the conditions that will affect the ball in flight*. So it is mightily important for the player to be aware of those conditions and understand how they affect his shot.

The job, then, of your inner caddie is to collect the data you need to make a successful shot. Most of us already collect some of that data: we try to find out how far away the target is in order to select the right club for the job. Most of us usually gauge the wind speed and direction, because we know that wind will affect our little 1.620-ounce ball in flight. If the lie of the ball is bad — buried in deep rough or sitting in a bunker — we'll usually take note of that, too.

The inner caddie, on the other hand, pays attention to *everything* — not just the wind direction, speed, and consistency, and the lie of the ball. He calculates which shots are makeable, and which are not, quickly sizing up no less than three different routes to the target: an aggressive line, a safer alternative, and a bail-out Plan C. He determines the no-go areas — the water hazards, the bunkers, the trees . . . the places from which up-and-downs are unlikely — and decides how they are to be avoided. He factors in his knowledge of "his player" — that is, himself — and which clubs he is comfortable hitting and which he is not.

Once all that data is collected, he then selects a shot that will give himself the opportunity to stand over the ball and swing with the utmost confidence. No golfer — whether a tournament professional or a 36-handicapper — should attempt to make a shot without feeling completely sure that he can make the shot happen. That's the kind of secret to success that will ultimately help him — and you — to win.

Facts, figures, and feel: Mike Weir and caddie analyzing all the conditions before making a decision on the shot.

# Chapter 3
## The Game Plan

"Think management. You want to always get your ball into 'the mayor's office,' the sweet spot on the fairway where you can attack the pins. Simple as that!"

*— George Lucas,*
*former caddie and "Father of the Yardage Book"*

# 3

## The Game Plan:
### Charting *Your* Course for the Win

During a practice round years ago, Bernhard Langer arrived at his ball in the fairway and asked his caddie, Brad Klein, what the yardage was for his approach shot to the green. Klein consulted his yardage book and told the player: "One hundred nineteen to the front, 125 to the pin." Langer asked his caddie how he knew this. Klein pointed to a nearby sprinkler head in the fairway and told his player he had paced off the distance from that point.

"Ah," Langer said, "But did you measure it from the front or the back of the sprinkler head?"

One hopes that Langer was just kidding, because a distance differential of merely five inches probably wouldn't make or break any golf shot except a putt. But it does demonstrate how touring pros leave almost nothing to chance when they prepare for a tournament. And how they depend on their caddies to gather *all* the facts about a course.

Thinking like a caddie begins long before a player steps onto the 1st tee. A great deal of "caddie work" takes place in advance of the round of golf, in the

David Duval zeroes in on a putt, with the help of his caddie.

Jason Bohn and his caddie each double-check their yardage books to get the right number.

form of forethought, preparation, course mapping, strategizing, and practice rounds.

Angelo Argea, Jack Nicklaus's longtime caddie, once wrote about his man's pregame preparations for a tournament. "Jack Nicklaus approaches a round of golf as if he were F. Lee Bailey entering a courtroom," Angelo wrote in his book *The Bear and I*. "Exhaustively prepared, with all the necessary data in his bag/briefcase. Meticulously equipped and attired. Systematic. Organized. Businesslike. He has it all down to a fine science."

Compare that approach to the typical one of the weekend golfer: arriving at the course just a few minutes before a tee time, running to the range to hit a few balls, dashing to the tee. Everything rushed, chaotic, out of control.

Of course, golf professionals and their caddies. have lots of time to do their prep work, including several days of practice and a Pro-Am tournament before the main event. And they play mostly the same courses year after year, leading to great familiarity with each course's quirks and corners. Ordinary golfers playing in a tournament at a new golf course probably don't have the time to scout that course with the same attention to detail a professional caddie would. However, many of us play at a "home course" or have local courses that we frequent time and again, so it should be possible to compile the necessary data just as a caddie would.

## GETTING THE LAY OF THE LAND

Even if you've played your home course a thousand times, however, and think you know every inch of its terrain, it will be helpful to take another look at it, this time through a caddie's eyes. Many courses these days sell yardage books, which will provide the basic data on what each hole looks like (including where the trouble is), as well as general yardage figures from various positions on the course. If you've never played the course before, these guides are a great help. Even better, however, is to construct your own yardage book, with information that is relevant just to your game. The yardage books carried by professional caddies for each course on tour are well-worn and annotated specifically for their player. They can use them year after year, unless Rees Jones has been called in for a renovation.

Having your own customized yardage book, then, is the first step towards thinking like a caddie, because it will reflect your game, your level of competence, and your specific game plan for beating the golf course and your opponents. Steve Williams, Tiger Woods's caddie, has yardage books that probably have lots of notes about where the troubles are for tee shots that fly

What was the plan? Phil Mickelson and Jim "Bones" Mackay review their notes.

## George Lucas — Father of the Yardage Book

Golfing lore says that Jack Nicklaus was the first professional golfer to chart every course he played, measuring the yardages and writing everything down in his yardage book. George Lucas begs to differ.

"Jack wasn't the first to do that, and he'd be the first to tell you so," says Lucas. "He was just the first player seen doing it on television, because he was in the lead so often. Ben Hogan and Sam Snead used to chart courses, too. In the old days, they'd just take a scorecard and make a note of how long it was to the fairway bunker, or where the trouble was around the green. It was just a lot simpler."

Lucas began his caddie career in 1974 in Palm Springs, when he hooked up with a young no-name pro, Bobby Walzel. They tried qualifying for the PGA Tour's Bob Hope Desert Classic, and missed by one stroke in the Monday qualifying event. In those days, however, there was a consolation tournament for those who missed out on the big-show tournament, and Walzel managed to win it that week. "That win got us into Riviera the next week and invited back to the Hope the following year. Bobby asked me if I wanted to carry for him and I said, 'What the hell.'"

The duo only lasted for another six months or so ("Bobby 'forgot' what he said he'd pay me," Lucas says with a chuckle) — so he found another bag and continued on for the next ten years or so, living the nomadic life of a tour caddie.

But as more and more of the PGA Tour pros, and their caddies, began to emulate Nicklaus's organized approach to the pro game, Lucas thought there might be a business in compiling and selling weekly yardage books to caddies and pros.

"I knew they had to be accurate above all," he says, "as well as easy to read and understand. In the heat of the moment, on the back nine on Sunday with the tournament at stake, they didn't need to be wondering if this was the right sprinkler head in the book or not."

Lucas started out by measuring courses with a pre-measured length of twine, which he used to determine distances from all fixed points on a golf course. But he soon found out that twine will stretch when it gets wet. "I learned that lesson when Lee Trevino began to holler at me across a fairway that the new book was off by a couple of yards," he says. He immediately purchased a surveyor's cable, in plastic, and modified it by measuring out ten-yard increments. "I used that for twenty years, until the laser devices came out. Sometimes I still use it."

His first purchase of a laser range guide was in 2000 when he began to chart the courses on the LPGA Tour as well. "The first one was a big old thing that sat on a tripod," he recalls. "The first week the thing fell over and broke and I was out about $1500." Now he uses the handheld laser devices, which can zero in on something and give an accurate read-out.

But he admits that just pacing off the yards is as good as any device. "Once you get a little practice, pacing is pretty accurate. I've tested myself against the laser and I'm usually within a yard."

Lucas says that of all the pros he's worked with, Andy Bean had the most accurate, deadeye reckoning skill. "Andy was the best. Amazing. He could look at a flagstick and say, 'It's 127 yards,' and he'd be right every time. He never used a yardage book, but his caddie sure did!"

These days, Lucas is taking it easy. He sold his yardage book business to The Stracka Line (www.strackaline.com) and does an occasional job measuring or remeasuring a course. But he still knows the most important thing any golfer needs: "Think management," he says. "You want to always get your ball into 'the mayor's office,' the sweet spot on the fairway where you can attack the pins. Simple as that!"

300 or 325 yards. Your yardage book should instead chart the troubles that await your usual tee shot of 200 or 225 yards. A bit later in this chapter, we'll get into the specifics of how to build your own custom yardage book.

Touring professionals, even though they rely on their caddies for accurate yardages, often maintain their own yardage books, just to make sure. "The caddies at professional events get yardage books and pin sheets, but nearly 100 percent will walk the golf course hole by hole and chart it," says Don Bobillo, longtime caddie coordinator at the Phoenix Open. "Knowing their player, they mark the landmarks. They prepare by walking the course, charting the landmarks, and getting it all down pat."

One year at Phoenix, Rocco Mediate was auditioning caddie Matt Achatz to take over the job as his fulltime looper. "He threw me under the bus," Matt recalled. "He had me clubbing him, reading greens. I realized it was a test."

Rocco remembers the moment when he knew Matt had passed that test. "It was the third hole at Phoenix," he says. "It's a long par 5, and I knew I couldn't reach it in 2. So I asked Matt for the yardage to the front left bunker and the front right. He said, 'Two hundred ten to the right, and 230 to the left. But why are you asking? There's 40 yards of fairway directly in front of the green.' That he understood my game instinctively like that sealed the deal for me."

The key to mapping and measuring a course, then, is not to just pace off the yardage from Point A to Point B, but to look at a golf course through the player's eyes. And since you are the player, your preparation work should involve mapping a course for only one person's game: yours. You can buy, or make, a yardage book that charts every inch of terrain. But what you need to win is a book of strategy that shows you *the best routes to take on every hole* so as to help you make a better score.

George Lucas first began caddying in 1974, and after several decades on the tour, began compiling and printing the "official" yardage books at each stop on the tour (see sidebar opposite page). He has charted and graphed most of the major courses in the country. His advice: Know what you got to get what you want! There's no sense in planning to hit a drive 300 yards if your Sunday best only goes 225.

PGA Tour player Phil Tataurangi considers himself a student of golf course architecture, believing a key to playing well on a particular course is to know the mind of the architect who designed it. "I like to 'read' a course with my caddie, Brendan Woolley, during the practice rounds prior to the start of a tournament," Tataurangi says. "We talk about the best strategy based on the design as well as factoring in all the conditions we expect to experience during the tournament." What all that preparation does is allow Tataurangi to put his game on "autopilot" and let his caddie feed him all the necessary information before each shot.

Yardage is not a strategy. It is merely the first bit of information used to develop one. Equally important to knowing the physical distances on a golf course is understanding the strengths and weaknesses of your own game. That requires an honest appraisal of your skills and knowing how far you can comfortably hit each club in your bag. Gil Morgan was once asked how far he could hit a 2-iron. "How far do I have to hit it?" he replied. His cryptic answer meant that he had the requisite skill to step it up (or down) to hit that club a variety of distances,

It says right here . . . Padraig Harrington listens as his caddie, Ronan Flood, reels off facts and figures.

in a variety of shape shots. If he needed to hit a 2-iron 210 yards with a high fade into a tucked pin, he could do that. Likewise, he could hit a low screamer under some tree branches so it could roll all the way onto a green 230 yards away. That's why he has his name embossed on a tour bag.

Those of us who play for fun instead of money don't have those same skills and shouldn't pretend that we do. Instead, you should know how far a normal, reasonably good shot should go with each of your clubs. Not a perfect shot — for as Dr. Bob Rotella told us in his book, *Golf is Not a Game of Perfect*, those are few and far between. Weekend golfers may hit two or three "perfect" shots in any given round; the rest are the typical collection of OK, semi-OK, reasonably good, fair, awful, terrible, and don't-ask! Use your OK shots — semi-OK to be conservative — and map your course and strategy with that data.

Remember, the point of the game is not proving one's manhood, but simply to get the ball into the hole in the least number of strokes. Eliminating doubles, triples, and "others" will reduce your scores. Kenny Harms, the caddie for PGA Tour pro Kevin Na, explains it this way: "Every hole on every course on the PGA Tour is a birdie hole for the pros. At the end of the day, the stats show that every hole has been birdied several times. You don't eliminate any scoring opportunities before the round begins. You have a sense of how that birdie would happen, including whatever risk is involved, and you let

## You Can Never Have Too Much Information

Bradley "The Professor" Klein's guide to mapping a course:

- Measure all fixed positions: sprinkler heads, bunkers, rocks, trees, cross hazards, water hazards . . . anything that's not going to move.

- Calculate and note all approach distances.

- Map out the entrance to the green, showing width of entry.

- Measure the length and width of the green and mark the center.

- From the tee: measure the distance to any fairway bunkers and hazards in play for you.

- Measure the layup distances on all par 5s. Find the area in front of the green that's your most comfortable wedge distance, and calculate the distance back to where your typical drive will land. Then be sure to mark the layup landing-area on your hole diagram.

- I always carried a compass so I knew where North was. I mapped every hole in advance and wrote down the wind direction for each day.

- I would walk the course backwards when mapping, always a good way to see the angles and understand the architect's preferred route to the hole.

the circumstances help you decide whether you are going to play for it. The amateur player has to think differently. He is going to be playing for the center of most greens. He can't legitimately try to shape the ball into a pin. What the amateur is looking for is easy pins — something he can shoot at and not be penalized for by missing a club long or short, or a slight pull or push. Most any tucked pin is a sucker pin for the weekend player, even the guys in the championship flight."

In other words, the pregame strategizing should include developing a plan of attack for every hole. For the long, tough holes, especially holes that always seem to give you the most trouble, plan to play conservatively and avoid big numbers. For the shorter holes, adopt a more aggressive attack. Develop a game plan that doesn't call for shots you don't have in your repertoire. If you have trouble hitting consistent 3-irons, try to avoid circumstances that call for those shots. Likewise, if your pitching and chipping game is strong, develop a strategy where you can use those shots often. Play to your strengths and avoid the weakest part of your game.

Brett Waldman, the current caddie for Camilo Villegas and a former looper for Ben Crane, thinks that pregame strategy is even more important for amateurs than it is for the pros who, again, have the shots and the experience to attack almost every hole. "Strategy for the amateur golfer should be more disciplined than for a tour player," he says. "The guy who shoots 80 should absolutely force himself to back off the driver two or three times every single round. I've watched amateurs play enough to feel strongly about that."

## BUILDING A STRATEGY BOOK

It should be obvious by now that you need your own yardage book. Perhaps your course already has one that you can purchase. If not, making your own is not that difficult. You can annotate a scorecard that has a diagram of the hole, purchase a small, spiral-bound notebook that fits in your back pocket, or simply use eighteen 3″ x 5″ index cards and staple them together. It doesn't have to be fancy . . . just relevant to your game.

A great way to get a very accurate rendering of your golf course is to go to Google Maps and enter the address. Once you have the location identified, click on "satellite" for a nice aerial view of the golf course. Use the zoom feature to get a detailed look at each hole and make your drawing from the satellite photos.

Use a pencil and sketch in the outline of each hole on your course. It doesn't have to be a work of art or one drawn to scale, just a simple drawing of the hole, showing the positions of bunkers, water hazards, doglegs, trees and bushes, rocky outcroppings, etc. You will also want to draw a diagram of the green, showing the shape, contours, and all the trouble that may surround it.

Once you've got the course drawn out, one hole to a page, then it's time to start measuring. In the sidebar on p. 51 are the recommendations of former caddie Bradley S. Klein, known as "The Professor." (Today, he has a Ph.D., teaches college-level courses, and also is the architecture editor for *Golfweek.*)

Caddies don't rely on anything that purports to represent an accurate yardage, be they 150-yard markers, bushes, or posts, and they usually double-check all marked sprinkler heads. They know the only way to be sure of a yardage is to measure it yourself, and often twice. Jack Nicklaus even sent his man Angelo out on the golf course before every round to check and step off the pin positions, even though the PGA Tour provides pin sheets showing the hole locations for every tournament round. Why? He didn't trust them to get the measurements right! Yes, that's Type-A behavior, but then again, Jack Nicklaus won more major tournaments that anyone else in history. Says Kevin Na's caddie, Kenny Harms, "Every once in a while there will be a sprinkler head that is seventy-six yards on the golf course but the book has it at sixty-seven yards. There are usually not too many errors like that, but you check everything you can."

Almost every caddie and player on tour today owns a laser range finder for mapping or checking yardages on a course. These handy little devices are invaluable and a great time-saver. (Remember: the use of range finders during a tournament is forbidden by the Rules of Golf.) If you don't have a range finder, then good old fashioned pacing off is the way to go. (Brad Klein says that he often used to visit a local baseball diamond and make sure that it took exactly thirty of his strides to cover the ninety feet between home plate and first base!). Many touring pros in the past also used measuring wheels during practice rounds to chart their preferred routes around a course.

The read begins: Andrew Magee studies the slope of the green after making a chip.

Just because you have a yardage book doesn't make you infallible. Don Bobillo, who has been affiliated with the Phoenix Open for more than forty years, where his primary responsibility has been coordinating caddies for the tournament and the Pro-Am, tells this story about Raymond Floyd. "One year, Raymond Floyd was playing the 1st hole and his second shot flew over the green. The caddie told Floyd he had hit the wrong club so Floyd asked to see the yardage book. It turned out that the caddie had the yardage book from the previous week's tournament. The caddie said, 'That's my fault. Now get it up and down.'"

Once you've got the basics of your course measured accurately, then you can begin to fill in the strategic elements relevant for your game. Your hole diagram should indicate the preferred landing area for your tee shot. It should show the prevailing wind direction, as well as the distance to carry or avoid fairway bunkers or hazards, or to reach the corner of a dogleg. The diagram should also indicate the distance to the far side of a dogleg.

With a sketch of the green, and especially the entrance to the green, your diagram should indicate the safest place to land on the putting surface. Determine the yardage to the center of the green, for that is where you will likely be aiming . . . not at some tucked pin. "I diagram the greens, writing in carry distances to various locations, then I add the slopes using lines and arrows," says Kenny Harms. "If there's a grain factor that's worth accounting for I will diagram the grain as well."

Make some notes about what lies beyond the green. Be sure to indicate the prevailing wind direction on your green diagram as well, as sometimes the green sits at a different angle than the tee box. You can then add in as much detail about the green as you prefer. Show the mounds and humps, draw arrows to indicate the direction of grain, make notes about bunkers with high lips, or areas surrounding the green with deep rough or sharp drop-offs.

If you play a course regularly, you should be familiar with the most popular hole locations on each green and their idiosyncrasies. Duly note them on your yardage book and refer to them before you play your shot into the green. For example, if one green has a particularly nasty pin placement where you absolutely cannot afford to be above the hole, note that on the green map and let it serve as a reminder when you are playing the hole and see the flag in that area. It will save you strokes in the long run.

Borrow the graphic conventions used by the television commentators when they show a helicopter overfly of a hole: the no-go areas are often superimposed with red Xs. Draw some of those on your hole diagrams — in red pencil — to remind yourself where you don't want to hit the ball.

Because you are now thinking like a caddie who is always upbeat and positive, you might also want to jot down some brief words of encouragement to yourself when you look at your yardage book on the tee. "Birdied this hole twice last year" or "Lots of room for driver" help instill positive thoughts in your head before you play the hole.

In any case, your new strategy book should indicate the preferred line you will play on each hole, the suggested clubs to use for each shot, and the best ways to avoid trouble along the way. Having such a guide in your pocket will not guarantee that you can play the course flawlessly, but it will remind you where on the course you can take chances, and where you need to play safely. It will help organize and strengthen your thinking process, and give you at least a road map for a better score.

Now all you have to do is go out and do it!

## IT'S IN THE BAG

The caddie's other main role in pregame preparation is to make sure the player's golf bag is ready for action. That means checking and cleaning the clubs, making sure all the necessary equipment is in the bag, and planning for the player's needs during the round.

Professional golfers use different equipment than ordinary weekend golfers. Their clubs have been bent and adjusted into custom lie-angles, their shafts are calibrated and "tuned" to deliver the best performance for their swing type and speed, and they are designed to provide the most detailed sensory feedback to the player. Clubs that weekend golfers play with are often bought off the shelf, and designed to make up for our less-than-perfect swings with perimeter weighting, flexible graphite shafts, oversized faces, and other technological advantages.

Still, the biggest difference between the pro's clubs and yours is something simple and nontechnological: the grips. "Grip maintenance is one area in which a great disparity exists between pros and amateurs," writes Mike Carrick, Tom Kite's longtime caddie, in his book *Caddie Sense*. "Most average players rarely clean their grips off and almost never change them. In contrast, I clean the grips thoroughly before every round, particularly when wet conditions exist. In addition, Tom changes his grips every three months. I always wipe down each grip with a damp towel before each round, leaving them feeling nice and tacky and allowing good control over the shot."

"Treat the equipment with a lot of respect and care," says caddie Kenny Harms. "If you watch tour caddies, we are constantly wiping the grips with a wet towel, then a dry towel. How often do amateur golfers do this? Pretty seldom. We do it many times a day. A tour player shouldn't ever put his hands on a grip that isn't nicely cleaned up."

So get out a damp cloth and get those grips cleaned! If it's been years since you changed them, do it before your next important round of golf or tournament. Your golf professional or a local golf shop can change out all your grips for a nominal fee, or you can buy new grips and change them yourself. Playing with new grips, or nicely cleaned and tacky grips, is one of those small things that can pay huge dividends.

Of course, caddies will also make sure the rest of the club is cleaned as well. "I polished Jack Nicklaus's irons until I could almost use one to shave with," Angelo Argea said. This means brushing the grooves to eliminate any dirt, and wiping the clubface down with a wet towel and then a dry one. It doesn't take much to send a golf ball off line, so it doesn't make much sense to play with dirty clubs.

In addition to clean clubs, make sure the bag contains anything else you might need for a round of golf: weather suit, extra gloves, an ample supply of balls, tees, and scorecard pencils.

Finally, make sure to include something to eat and drink during the round. Most amateur golfers overlook nutrition on the golf course, a major mistake. Playing a round of golf is a physical activity that takes up to five hours, and the human body needs fuel and fluid during that time. Pack some energy bars, bananas, apples, or other snacks, and make sure you have plenty of water. Good nutrition during golf usually does not include eating a hot dog and quaffing a cold beer at the turn, despite the longstanding traditions in American golf!

Tiger Woods often reaches into his bag during a round for a peanut butter sandwich, a good source of instant energy. Seve Ballesteros, for one, always liked to munch on an apple. During one round, Seve, always infamous for being tough on his caddies, once complained to his then-looper that the apple was too soft. "What am I, your caddie or a greengrocer?" the caddie responded. He was fired after the round!

The good news is that you can't fire yourself. But preparing for your round like a caddie — developing your personal game plan, and making sure your equipment is in good working order — is the best way to shave those all-important strokes off your score.

# Chapter 4
## Prep for Success

"There are only two ways to play: competitively and for fun.
If you want to play competitively, you have to practice. If you
want to play for fun, don't even keep score."

— *Bobby Verwey,*
*caddie and nephew of Gary Player*

# 4

## Prep for Success:
## Why Warming Up Matters

Golf, despite the presence of motorized carts and a cold beer at the turn, is an athletic endeavor. To perform at its best, your body needs to loosen up. All those big muscles, which have spent the week stuck behind a desk, need to get warm and limber.

Your inner caddie knows that you need some time before an important round of golf to get loose and warmed up. How long? That depends on you, the player. Kenny Harms has been a caddie on various pro circuits for many years, working for players as diverse as Aaron Baddeley, Michelle Wie, Teresa Lu and, most recently, Kevin Na on the PGA Tour. "All the tour players I've caddied for have a slightly different pattern of how much time they spend warming up before a round and what sequence they follow," says Harms. "My current boss, Kevin Na, warms up for ninety minutes. Hubert Green took sixty minutes, and Hale Irwin took forty-five minutes. Everyone warms up at their own speed, and the older one gets, the longer it takes to get loose. They were consistent on that, as long as there were no unusual circumstances. If you play tournaments at your club fairly often, pay attention to what your comfortable warm-up time is. Allow that amount of time and don't get distracted."

Michelle Wie gets some green advice from her father and then-caddie, B.J. Wie.

## Caddie Stretch — Getting Loose in 10 Minutes

The professional tours have everything a player needs, including a fitness van used by players to work out, warm up, and otherwise maintain their fitness. Before a tournament round, many players head for the fitness van as part of the warming-up process.

Here's a ten-minute series of exercises designed to get the body in shape for a round of golf:

### 90/90 Hamstring Stretch

- Lie down, your back flat on the floor, and your knees bent comfortably.

- Hold your leg just above the left knee with both hands and pull it back into the chest.

- Then straighten the leg upwards until you feel the tension in the hamstring muscles. Hold for 30 seconds.

- Repeat using your right leg. Do a series of repetitions, alternating legs until the hamstrings are loose.

### Glute Stretch

- Sit on the floor with your legs stretched out in front of your body. Bend the right knee up 90 degrees while keeping the hips facing forward. Place your hands on the floor slightly in front of your hips.

- Slowly press the upper torso forward into the right knee, keeping the hips facing forward. Keep pressing until you feel a slight stretch and tension in the right gluteus. Hold for 30 seconds.

- Repeat using your left leg. Do a few repetitions, alternating between your right and left legs.

### Standing Calf Stretch

- Standing on the floor, place your hands on your hips, and body leaning forward. Extend your left leg backwards until it is straight, toe on the floor, and bend the right knee slightly.

- Press your body weight forward and bend the right knee until tension is felt in your left calf. Hold this position for 30 seconds.

- Repeat, extending your right leg backwards and bending your left leg.

These three exercises will help get the big muscles limbered up for a successful round.

Getting loose is an important first step in winning golf.

## IF YOU WANT TO RIDE THE BIRDIE TRAIN . . .

A warm-up routine should include more than hitting a bunch of balls. Stretch out the big muscles of the legs and trunk. Swing a weighted club, or hold two or three irons together and swing them slowly to stretch out the shoulder and arm muscles. Do some trunk work, deep-knee bends, leg lifts, whatever you need to get loose. (See sidebar on p. 62 for a specific stretching regimen). On the tour, caddies often assist their players with stretching before a round. You'll have to make do with bracing yourself against the golf cart, or enlisting the help of a buddy.

Now, once your muscles are warmed up, ask yourself one very important question:

*What am I doing here?*

No, that's not a Zen koan, it's a serious question. What is your goal for hitting balls for the next thirty minutes or so? Mike Carrick, who caddied for Tom Kite for twenty years on the tour, said his player never went to the practice range without a goal and a purpose for the session in mind. Of course, Kite was one of the original grinders, who often spent hours beating balls on the range, trying to get each swing perfect. But Carrick, a native of Canada who taught physical education for a couple of years before the travel bug hit, also said that golfers who just go to the range and flail away are rarely found riding the birdie train!

The answer to your question is simple: I'm here to warm up for my round of golf. That is the only reason for going to the practice range before a round. Once you've decided on the purpose for visiting the practice range, follow through on it! Probably the worst thing you can do before an important round of golf is to beat a hundred balls, or go through the bag making sure each club is "working." Save the practicing for a practice session.

Eli Brown has worked as a caddie at the venerable Seminole Golf Club in Jupiter, Florida, for several decades. He's watched both good and bad players warm up. "I think players should start with short shots with a sand wedge, pitching wedge, or 9-iron and then work up through a few of the other irons," he says. "End with the long clubs: 5-wood, 3-wood, and the driver. After that, hit a few bunker shots

# So You Wanna Be Like Tiger?

### TIGER'S WORKOUT REGIMEN AT THE GYM:

Tiger Woods is a physical fitness buff. He's also the best conditioned professional golfer in history (power-lifter Frank Stranahan was an avowed amateur golfer, who played in major golf championships in a career than spanned from 1936 to 1954).

How does he do it? Here's his workout routine:

1. **Cardio.** He spends 30 minutes in the morning running, riding a bike, or on a treadmill.

2. **Stretching.** He pays attention to leg and trunk muscles while warming up.

3. **Core.** Keeping the torso in place, he works on his limbs, always focusing on posture and balance. This also helps the big muscles of the abdomen and back, needed for golf's twisting motion.

4. **Power.** Get those sneakers on! Tiger runs either speed bursts of 3 miles or endurance runs of 7 miles. Or so.

5. **Strength.** In the gym, he'll do bench presses, shoulder presses, and squats.

6. **Cool.** More stretching as he cools down helps keep the muscles from tightening up.

Doing the tango? Nope, just stretching the back muscles.

## A DAY IN TIGER'S LIFE

Why is Tiger Woods the world's best golfer? Take a look at his typical daily schedule and workout routine. This is what he does at least six days a week, except when he's playing in (and winning) golf tournaments:

| | | |
|---|---|---|
| 6:00 | a.m. | Weight workout (90 minutes) |
| 7:30 | a.m. | Breakfast |
| 8:00 | a.m. | Practice tee (2 hours) |
| 10:00 | a.m. | Putting green |
| 10:30 | a.m. | Play 9 holes |
| 12:00 | p.m. | Lunch |
| 1:00 | p.m. | Practice tee (2 hours) |
| 3:00 | p.m. | Short game work |
| 4:00 | p.m. | Play 9 holes |
| 5:00 | p.m. | Putting green |
| 5:30 | p.m. | Home |

"After we finish this hole, we get to run five miles!"

"My game is so bad I gotta hire three caddies — one to take the left rough, one for the right rough, and one down the middle. And the one down the middle doesn't have much to do."
— professional golfer Dave Hill

and then head for the putting green." This warm-up recipe makes the most sense and is utilized by most of the players on the PGA Tour.

When you start with a sand or pitching wedge, you can make some long, easy swings that will help you find a good tempo for the day. Start by hitting half-power shots, concentrating only on keeping the swing smooth and trying to hit each shot solidly, in the center of the clubface.

Imagine your caddie standing at your side encouraging you with words like slow, easy, smooth, effortless, and oily. ("I try to get 'oily,'" states Sam Snead in his autobiography, Slammin' Sam. "Oily means a smooth motion. It's the feeling that all your bones and muscles are so in sync, any movement you make is going to be smooth and graceful.") With your first few swings, you shouldn't aim at anything or worry about where or how far the ball goes. It should all be about tempo and connection.

After you get a good tempo down with the half-wedges, then you can stretch out to a full swing, trying to keep the same tempo in place. "Amateur golfers who are getting ready for a tournament should spend just enough time hitting full shots to get the rust off," says Kevin Fasbender, caddie for Rory Sabbatini. Work through the bag, but don't hit so many shots that you get fatigued. Save your energy for when it counts, on the golf course.

Before moving on to the long clubs — fairway woods and driver — go back and hit a few more easy wedge shots. That same long and easy tempo will help with the distance clubs. Make sure to hit at least as many 3-woods off a tee as drivers, since it's likely your strategic plan will have you using that club a lot during the round.

The pros will spend some time in a warm-up hitting their money clubs: drivers, which they need to get into the fairway, and wedges and shorter irons with which they can zero in on a pin. Amateurs should do the same thing, but their money clubs are much different. "The major amount of time in the warm-up session should be spent chipping and putting, " says Fasbender. "That's where the tournament is going to be won or lost — around the green."

Teammates Brad Faxon (front) and Fred Couples look for the break.

Caddie, A.J. Montecinos Jr., confers on a shot with his player, PGA champion Y.E. Yang.

It's true, all the short-game strokes, chipping, pitching, and putting account for more than 40 percent of one's total score. Whacking the big club may be fun, but getting up and down from just off the green will lower your scores dramatically. And isn't that the point of the whole game?

> "There are only two ways to play: competitively and for fun. If you want to play competitively, you have to practice. If you want to play for fun, don't even keep score."
> — Bobby Verwey, caddie and nephew of Gary Player

Make sure to hit at least a half-dozen shots from the practice bunker. Chances are you'll end up in one during the round. Likewise, hit a few greenside chips, or a few little pitch shots. These are all important shots you'll likely face during the round, and being prepared to get up and down from off the green will save several strokes.

Amateur golfers who watch a PGA Tour practice round will notice that caddies and players do a lot of extra practicing when they get to a green. "We look at all the different areas of the green where we will have putts and chips of different angles," says Timmy Goodell, caddie for Nick Watney for the last six years. In a twenty-year caddie career, Goodell has also looped for Russ Cochran, Lee Janzen, Blaine McCallister, and Robin Freeman. He hooked up with Watney when his player was still a wannabe on the Nationwide Tour. "During the practice round we will rehearse various scenarios for getting up and down based on the four cup positions for the week," he says.

Most golfers like to end their warm-up session on the putting green. In a later chapter, we'll see how caddies go about reading greens, but on the practice green before a round, most caddies let their players work by themselves.

But just like the warm-up session on the range, warming up on the putting green should involve getting a sense of the speed of the greens and honing a nice, relaxed putting stroke. It should not be all about sinking putts (or worrying about *not* sinking putts). Make the session all about process rather than results.

## THE AIM OF A GOOD PUTTING WARM-UP

A good way to start off is to hit your first practice putts at anything other than a hole. Aim at a distant leaf, discolored spot, or even the edge of the green across the way and try to see your putts stopping near that aiming point. This exercise will quickly show you how fast the greens are running and help you get your stroke tuned into the speed.

A secondary goal for the putting-green session is to make sure you're hitting the ball squarely with the putter — not on the toe or heel — and that you're releasing the putter through the ball and not decelerating. There are many kinds of drills designed to help with contact and release. But again, your goal for putting warm-ups should be to get a feel for the greens and for your stroke.

The final part of the putting warm-up is reinforcing confidence. Professional golfers will work on making their money putts — usually in the five- to ten-foot range — and not leave the green until they've sunk a few in a row. Your money putt is the three-footer, often the difference between a par and a bogey, or a bogey and worse. Before you leave the green, then, take the hole marker out of one of the practice holes on the green and give yourself a fairly straight three-footer. Once you've made three or four in a row, that's it . . . you're done.

Don't leave the green until you've made at least one short putt. If you have to (remember, your group is waiting on the tee for you!) then shorten your putt down to a foot or so. Just make one, listen for the rattle of the ball in the cup, and anchor the feeling and sound of a good putt. Take that feeling and sound with you onto the course and plan to hear it often during the round.

Now that you're loose and limber, and have rehearsed your tempo, ball striking, bunker play, short-game strokes, and your putting, it's time for one last check-in with your inner caddie. Count the clubs one more time, double-check to make sure you've got everything in the bag you'll need for the round and have something to eat and drink to keep your energy levels up.

Finally, find a moment to review the game plan one more time. Pull out your strategy book and go through the course. Check to see if the wind direction is unusual or follows your notes on the prevailing conditions. Find out if any weather patterns are expected that could change the conditions on the course. Remind yourself of the holes that are to be played with care, and those where you've planned to attack.

"After playing a round with Gary Player during the U.S. Open at Seminole, Ben Hogan said, 'You'll be a great player. Do you practice hard?' Yes, he did, Player said. Hogan replied, 'Double it.'"
— Bobby Verwey, caddie and nephew of Gary Player

"You always have to factor in how a guy's feeling on any given day," says Steve Williams, Tiger Woods's caddie. "When he gets to the golf course and he's been on the range, you can see if he's confident today or if he's a bit iffy. I'll know before we start if he's swinging good or not today, and with all the other variables, I'll know what kind of day to expect. It's not good going to the 1st hole and trying to pull off a miracle." Those observations should go into the final plan for the day.

If you've done your preparation well, developed a winning plan, and warmed up all aspects of your game, you should be able to head for the 1st tee with

confidence and anticipation for a great round to come. The golfer who is prepared and has a plan will have an advantage over those who don't. The golfer who believes in his strategy and plans to execute it one stroke at a time will play with more confidence, and be less distracted by the occasional glitches sure to crop up, and will almost certainly score better.

Practice with the purpose of playing better golf.

# Chapter 5

## It's Element-ary!

"The wind always helps the golfer. No matter the direction, no matter what shot. And a strong wind helps more than a lighter wind."

*— Nick Faldo,*
*Masters and British Open champion*

# 5

## It's Element-ary!

Brent Everson, who has caddied for several players on the PGA Tour, relates the normal check-list of information he provides to his player, Justin Leonard, for every shot. "He'll want to know how the shot is playing. How the wind will affect it. How firm the green is, what we need to allow for the release into the green once the ball lands. Where exactly we need to land it at what distance, where we want our golf ball to end up in relation to the pin on the green, etc. . . . ."

As you can see, there are a lot more pieces of data to consider than just the yardage distance. Everson, like most professional caddies, has to take a quick inventory of all the relevant elements on every shot, and be ready to answer all those questions if his player should ask.

Foremost among those elements are the following:

- **The wind** and how it will affect the next shot.

- **The weather:** rain, cold, or other factors that might affect a ball's flight.

At the Ryder Cup, intense pressure is one of the elements considered by Sergio Garcia and his caddie.

- **The lie:** Not only is the ball lying cleanly, but are there terrain considerations?

- **The stance:** Will the position of the feet affect the way the shot must be played?

- **The circumstance:** Is there drama or tension in the unfolding competitive situation that might add nerves or adrenalin to the shot?

The weekend golfer often does not take all these elements into consideration with quite as much exactitude as tour pros do — but knowing what the players and caddies on tour know can always help. Here are some of their more subtle insights:

Observing the flight of his ball, former major winner Larry Nelson and his caddie, Russ Craver, take note of the wind's effect.

## GONE WITH THE WIND

After an accurate yardage reading, knowing what the wind is doing is the single most important consideration in sizing up a golf shot. Whether a gentle zephyr or a full-blown gale, the wind has the potential to affect every golf shot from a 300-yard drive to a three-foot putt.

In dealing with a windswept golf course, one great place for the skilled (or not-so-skilled) amateur to start is with an attitude adjustment. It comes courtesy of Masters and British Open champion Nick Faldo. In the words of Sir Nick: "The wind always helps the golfer. No matter the direction, no matter what shot. And a strong wind helps more than a lighter wind."

Here's an example of what Faldo means: "If you've got a 150-yard shot straight into a good, steady breeze, you're going to take a 6-iron instead of a 7-iron. Based on the yardage, you've now got too much club. But your friend the wind is going to help that 6-iron shot drop to the ground twelve or fifteen yards shorter than it normally would."

Sure it's all in the mind — but where else is golf played? It's a simple matter of looking at the wind as a helpful influence rather than a hindrance. "When you look at things that way," says the wily Faldo, "wind play gets much easier and more enjoyable."

Extending Faldo's logic, a left-to-right cross breeze will help the off-line shot you play toward

### No Such Things as a One-Club Wind?

The late club pro and respected teacher Billy Mitchell was fond of saying that the "one-club wind" didn't exist. Mitchell, longtime head professional at Innis Arden Golf Club in Old Greenwich, Connecticut, was talking about upwind iron shots and his own preference for playing them via the "knock down" method.

The technique for a knock-down iron shot is to close your stance a bit, grip the club with the clubface slightly shut, position the ball back in your stance and make firm, crisp contact with a shortened swing. (You close the clubface slightly because, with the ball back in your stance, you are making contact earlier in your stroke, before the face has a chance to square up.)

If Mitchell was playing from his normal 8-iron distance into a wind that normally calls for one extra club, he would take his 6-iron, not his 7-iron, then strike the shot with the throttled-back swing a knockdown iron shot requires. "You add one club for the wind, itself," he told his students, "and one for the fact that you are not swinging with full force." The result would be a lower-flying shot that held its trajectory, landed short of the target, and ran up into scoring position obediently.

the green work back to the hole. And, obviously, the pitching wedge you play downwind from 130 yards is going to be helped along with ten more yards of carry.

How is wind measured and judged? Despite all the tearing and tossing of grass that golfers do, many tour caddies dismiss that technique as unhelpful. Leonard Ciccone, a PCA Hall of Fame caddie based in Montclair, New Jersey, looks to the treetops for a read on wind velocity. No movement up there means zero wind effect on the golf shot; a light waving motion means minimal effect; and vigorous back-and-forthing of the tree tops tells him to pull one less or one more club for the shot.

Ciccone also evaluates wind strength based on what direction it's blowing from. His decades on the bag have taught him that a warm southwest wind at ten miles per hour will affect golf shots less than a cooler wind — of the same speed — out of the northwest. Ciccone explains: "The moisture and density of those two winds [are] different," at least in his part of the world. As for tossing torn grass blades in the air, Ciccone will do it only to assess a tailwind. He's not sure why, only that long experience bears out the belief.

Heath Holt, who caddies for PGA Tour player John Rollins, advises the weekend golfer to learn from a fellow competitor's club selection and how his ball looks in flight — without slowing down play. "Sometimes you are going to want to know how the wind affects another player's ball flight. What we do on tour is get our club selection down to one or two clubs, and we'll talk about what we're watching for. If it looks like the other guy's shot got helped by the wind, we'll go with the weaker-lofted club. If it looks like it was held up, we'll go with the stronger club. But we're basically ready, with just one last, quick conversation that produces a final decision."

In a strong headwind, Hall of Fame caddie Dee Darden suggests a double adjustment for the amateur golfer — add a club and go conservative with your target. Darden, born on a North Carolina peanut farm in 1929 as the eighth of nine children, began caddying as soon as he could shoulder a bag. On long approaches upwind, he would counsel his players not to add two clubs and shoot at the pin, but rather to add one and play for a spot right in front of the green. "That way you've snuck past the wind, you're not in a hazard, and your next shot will be a little chip that the wind won't affect in any way," says Darden.

Nick Faldo reminds caddie and player alike that warmup time is all the more valuable on a day when the winds are whipping. "That's your chance to work the wind by experimenting with little adjustments," he says. "Hit iron shots choking down a half-inch and have your caddie check the distance you're getting. Choke down a full inch, taking full swings every time. Move the ball back in your stance. If there's a big tailwind, grip it way up on the top of the handle — and track your results."

## THE PRESSURE IS ON

It might seem like overkill to tell the weekend golfer to check the barometric pressure before going out to play in an important tournament or event. But serious golfers and their caddies leave no stone unturned in the search to save strokes.

The relative humidity in the air does affect — albeit slightly — the flight of a golf ball. If the air is very humid, like just before a storm breaks, or if there's a layer of fog, the ball won't carry quite as far as it would in drier air. While those conditions exist, a caddie would recommend going down a club to compensate for the reduced distance.

If you're reading this book at sea level, and you plan to play all your golf there, you can avoid having to include high altitude as a factor in carry distance. Josh White, a club professional in the Arizona mountains who has caddied in major championships, says high-elevation play can be fun, but complicated.

"If there are several different conditions affecting how your shot will carry, it's that one extra factor that makes you almost want to pull out a calculator," says White, of the acclaimed Forest Highlands Golf Club in Flagstaff, Arizona. On standard shots, he adds about 10 percent to sea level yardage. Caddying for a high-ball hitter, he would add even a touch more than 10 percent to the expected carry. "What gets you is playing in wind, having a downhill shot from a flyer lie — plus the thin air at altitude," says White. "You have to subtract ten yards, add fifteen, add ten then maybe add ten more. Then you have to commit to the shot." The caddie's job includes enforcing that commitment with decisive encouragement.

## RAIN DAYS

Most weekend golfers will cancel if the weather turns bad. But when a tournament rolls around, the game must go on, despite bad weather. When playing in a steady, soaking rain, the player and his inner caddie must work together to minimize the effect of it. That means a big umbrella to help keep golfer and clubs as dry as possible, and extra towels for the hands, the clubs, and especially the grips.

Pete McCann, who had done some caddying for Sam Snead, recalls that Snead didn't mind the rain whereas other tour players let it bother them. In the modern era, with so much high-tech, rain-resistant gear, any golfer can become a rain-tolerant Sam Snead-type by hustling to dry the grips and heads of each club after a shot.

Rainy days and Mondays: Fred Funk's caddie, Mark Long, keeps his man dry.

But rain is also a consideration in shot selection. "If you're really bundled up against a cold rain," says McCann, "you have to figure an extra club on longer shots. Your ball is just not going to carry as far, due to the impeded swing from having all those extra clothes on."

Cold weather is another distance killer. And it's not just the equipment that sometimes needs warming up. "The caddie has to check how far his player's shots are carrying during the warm up and note whether the weather is affecting his normal yardage," said Brent Henley, caddie for the forty-five-year-old Woody Austin. "Typically I'll see that he is shorter than normal, and usually that's a matter of his body just not being loose. A player of Woody Austin's age just doesn't get his normal carry on shots when it's early in the morning, or it's cold, or both. I have to adjust until he is finally loose, and that may be a little bit into the actual round."

## LIES, DAMNED LIES, AND BAD LIES

When you watch a golf tournament on television, you always hear the booth announcers asking the on-course reporter walking with the golfers, "What kind of lie does he have?" It's a question your inner caddie should ask about every shot, even those from the middle of the fairway.

How does the ball lie? Is it "clean," i.e., will you be able to deliver the clubface into the back of the ball without a layer of grass or anything else getting in the way? Is it "tight?" or sitting nakedly on a hard piece of ground? Is it nestled down into the rough and will that surrounding grass get in the way of the club as it tries to swish through on the way into the ball?

All of these types of conditions will affect how you determine a plan for the next shot. On a deep lie in the rough, you may not be able to execute the shot you want to play and will have to adjust to a more lofted shot to get back into play. Other lies will affect shots in other ways that you need to think about.

## TAKING A STANCE

Most weekend golfers also don't pay enough attention to their stance in any given shot. But this, too, must be factored in when sizing up a shot and its possibilities.

Professionals spend a lot of time on the practice range. Then they spend a lot of time off it. Indeed, on a golf course, with its changes in terrain, some natural and some installed by a diabolical architect, it's a rare treat to be able to play a shot from the same kind of nice, flat, perfect lies found on the practice tee. So the pros go off-road to practice other kinds of stances: sidehill, uphill, and downhill.

For right-handed players, when the ball is above your feet on a shot it will tend to curve from right to left. A ball played below your feet will tend to curve the other way, from left to right. A shot played in an upward-sloping stance tends to fly higher into the air and land a bit shorter than a flat-level shot; and a shot hit from a downhill stance tends to come out a bit lower and hotter as the hill delofts the club.

It should be obvious that collecting all these various bits of data can be done quickly, usually with the first look upon arriving at the ball. And no golfer should drag his heels and keep his playing partners waiting while he phones in for a weather report, gets out his surveying equipment to see how many degrees of slope there are, or goes rifling through an instructional book to remind himself how to hit a ball off a sidehill hanging lie!

So while acknowledging that slow play is a bane of all our existences, it is important to gather as many facts about the upcoming shot as one can. As you play the round, you should begin to know where the wind is coming from and how the weather is affecting golf shots on that particular day by being alert to your total environment and how others are playing. You should be able to size up the lie and stance with a glance, remembering to factor in any possible influences as you choose the right club for the shot.

Finally, it is important to be ever-mindful of the situation. A player who knows he's finishing back in the pack will keep to his original game plan on every hole. But a contending player may have to increase or decrease the amount of risk he takes, based on his position in the competition or his match. It's important not to substitute a tentative swing for a conservative club choice. "Plan conservatively, execute aggressively" is a phrase often heard at the game's top levels.

In those pressure situations, club selection may have to change based on surges of adrenaline, which can yield a 5-iron carry from a 6-iron shot. Bobby Brown, caddie for PGA Tour player Dustin Johnson, knows that scenario well. "Hitting good shots and good putts and being in contention is going to get the player and the caddie very pumped up," says Brown. "It will eventually add distance to one of your shots, and both you and the player need to be ready for that. On tour it generally doesn't happen until the last hour or so on Sunday, but you have to watch your player and guess right on when the adrenaline rush is coming."

When you're the one doing the playing, keep in mind that as you come down the stretch your distance will start to pick up, and adjust accordingly.

Caddies uniformly insist that a golfer cannot have too much information in planning a golf shot. Taking a moment to survey all the elements is how caddies provide an invaluable service to the player. Taking the time to do the same when you are sizing up a golf shot is an important way to make sure you're thinking like a caddie.

Wind, weather, speed of the course: the caddie keeps his eye on the ball.

# Chapter 6
## The Name of the Game Is Strategy

"Don't try to make shots you don't have."

— *Matt Achatz,*
*caddie for Rocco Mediate*

# 6

## The Name of the Game Is Strategy

Rocco Mediate, who took Tiger Woods into overtime at the 2008 U.S. Open at Torrey Pines, has ample experience with amateur golfers, whom he sees and plays with weekly at the tour's Pro-Am tournaments.

"They want to write checks with their clubs that their bodies just can't cash," Rocco says. His caddie, Matt Achatz, translates: "Don't try to make shots you don't have."

It is a constant temptation for weekend golfers to attempt to do things on a golf course that they just can't do, whether it is trying to bend the ball one way or the other, hit a certain club a certain distance, make a miraculous recovery, get up and down from an impossible lie, or consistently sink long putts.

In Chapter Three, you learned how to build an effective yardage book by creating a plan to get around your course based on an honest evaluation of your individual skills and knowledge. Once you're actually out on the course, playing the game, it is imperative that you stick to your game plan. This means you must approach each shot with three things in mind:

Bones Mackay knows his man, Phil Mickelson, likes to go for broke on pressure shots.

- Accurately evaluate the elements and conditions that will affect the shot.

- Decide on a course of action based *on those current elements* and your game plan, not on past history.

- Choose the shot that has the best chance of success.

Just because you are a weekend or occasional golfer doesn't mean you are fated to shoot your handicap, or worse. "I've taken solid 12 handicappers around a golf course in 76 or 77," says Achatz. "It wasn't because they played any better than their handicap; they just listened to me and didn't try to make any heroic shots."

Phil Tautarangi is another tour player who has observed his many Pro-Am partners. He is often amused at the decision-making of his amateur partners who are often highly successful corporate CEOs. "Assessing risk and reward is how many of them became successful in business," Tautarangi says. "But out on the golf course they seem to have forgotten everything they learned about risk back at the office. Golf is a great game, but a difficult game to play well, and a key component of playing good golf is understanding your limitations and playing within them."

Caddies understand that one of their main duties is to help their players get around the course in as few strokes as possible, no matter how. If a player is having a horrible day, a caddie would recommend using a putter for every shot if that is the only way to advance the ball safely down the fairway.

Amateur golfers, on the other hand, either vastly overrate their own talents or they simply choose to use a club because they think it's the one they're "supposed to use." Standing on a tee, many think the driver is the only possible club choice. In a bunker? Gotta use the sand wedge. One hundred and fifty from the pin? That's a 7-iron, no matter what.

Caddies and their players approach the game differently. Every shot is a new opportunity and a new challenge. Solving that challenge requires clear thinking, calm assessment, and fact-based decision-making. From the tee, the challenge is to get the ball to the position in the fairway that allows the easiest shot to the green, whether that means selecting the driver or an easy 5-iron. From the fairway, the challenge is to get the ball onto the green and hopefully close to the pin. That requires an assessment of the distance, wind conditions, lie, and situation, combined with the desire to avoid any and all greenside trouble: bunkers, sand, rough, etc. Having considered all the data, caddies and players will choose the club that will get the job done with the least amount of effort.

Of course, professional golfers are not like the rest of us. They have hit millions of practice balls, played thousands of golf holes in all kinds of conditions, and taken instruction from the world's best teachers. They also play with the finest equipment known to man, tweaked and adjusted to fit their personal specifications. And yet they still mess up fairly frequently. Even Tiger Woods.

The weekend golfer should not play a round expecting to bomb drives 300 yards or more, or think he'll be able to hit a 7-iron 175 yards, or get a wedge approach to bounce twice and stop on a dime. Nor should he expect to hit every shot perfectly during a round. Instead, he should have a strategy and a game plan that fits his level of capability, and then play to that plan. That is the only strategy that will result in fewer strokes.

Let's work our way around the course and see how this strategy plays out in real time.

## THE TEE — STEP AWAY FROM THAT DRIVER!

Most weekend golfers will reach for their driver as soon as they arrive at the tee of any of the long holes. It's reflexive — gotta pound one out here, you think — it's the traditional driving club, and it could be the absolutely *wrong* selection for that hole. When you're thinking like a caddie, there are no automatic decisions in club selection, no reference to what you hit here last time, or what club your opponent is using. Each shot is considered by itself and is informed by the conditions that exist at that particular moment in time.

The player-caddie team is constantly working collaboratively to share information and perspectives: when the player reaches the tee on a hole he consults his yardage book (or his memory) to double-check the location of his target — the place where he wants his tee shot to end up. In the meantime, the caddie is checking the wind conditions, and looking at his own yardage book to calculate the distances required to avoid or to cover the trouble —

"Top players never get flustered."
— Bobby Verwey, caddie and nephew of Gary Player

fairway bunkers, water hazards, protruding woods, or the short and long corners of a dogleg. The two will then get together and discuss the possible options for the shot. It doesn't matter to either caddie or player how long or short the hole is, where they stand in the tournament, or what the gallery will think of their club selection. They have a common goal: to get the ball into the part of the fairway that provides the best opportunity to get the next shot onto the green (or, on a par 5, near the green).

As a player thinking like a caddie, the first step is to select your target. Looking at your strategy book, you'll see the portion of the fairway you've selected as the optimum landing area, "the mayor's office," as former caddie George Lucas likes to call it. It is the area you've selected as that point on the fairway that will give you the best look at the green, the best angle to approach it, or the spot where you can hit the most comfortable (for you) club. Standing on the tee, you should zero in on the target. Make your target as tightly defined as possible. Instead of generic targets, such as "left side of fairway," or "right at that tree," focus in on a specific point in the fairway — a leaf, a shadow, a pattern in the mown grass. Block out everything else in your mind except that selected spot. You might even say it out loud — "I'm going to hit this shot to the edge of that shadow from that maple tree that's in the left center of the fairway." After all, when a caddie and his player are discussing a shot, they do it out loud and agree verbally on the target. Your playing partners might look at you funny, or think you're trying to call your shot à la Babe Ruth, but verbalizing your specific target can really help anchor it solidly in your mind.

Now, revert back into caddie mode. Your yardage book should indicate the distance to your target. Ask yourself the following crucial questions:

- What is the wind speed and in what direction is it blowing?

- How will that affect this shot?

- Are there other conditions at play here, like heavy air or rain?

- Is it uphill or down?

- What kind of shot do you envision? A high floater that will come down softly, or a low screamer that will hit and roll?

- Where are the no-go areas and what is the best way to avoid them: hit it over, keep it short of, or play away from them?

See the caddie checklist on p. 94 for other important questions to consider as well.

Of course, in order to avoid slow play and irritating your playing partners, you shouldn't take a lot of extra time to run through this checklist. Hopefully, having predetermined your strategy for each hole, you already have a pretty good idea of what you want to do with this shot, how far you need to hit it, and which club you believe will get the job done. Be sure, however, to take the time to consider the wind conditions. Other than the spin on the ball you yourself impart, any wind will always have an influence on the flight of your ball. A golf ball, remember, weighs just 1.620 ounces, roughly the same as eight sheets of 8.5″ x 11″ paper. It doesn't take much of a breeze to affect its flight in midair.

Rich Beem and his caddie, Billy Heim, line up a putt: lag it close or pour it in?

Once all the data have been reviewed, you'll get a clear picture of the proper club for this shot. Maybe it's a nice calm day, the fairway is wide open, trouble is scarce, and booming the driver is the proper choice. Maybe your goal is to just move the ball 200 yards to set up a good look at the green, and the 3-wood is the selection. Perhaps you're confronted with a small target surrounded by trouble, or with very windy conditions, and the smart play is an iron off the tee.

There are, of course, dozens of ways to play any golf hole, and there is no such thing as the "right" way to play it. Conditions vary from day to day: one day the wind may be helping on the hole, the next it may be against the player or blowing more from side to side. The only criterion for deciding how to play a shot is to choose the *easiest* one that will deliver the ball to your target. Pry your white fingers from their death-grip on the driver and look at this shot — and every other one — all by itself, objectively. Brett Waldman, caddie for several tour players, including Camilo Villegas, puts his finger on the problem: "Strategy for the amateur golfer should be more disciplined than for a tour player," he says. "The guy who shoots 80 should absolutely force himself to back off the driver two or three times every single round. I've watched amateurs play enough to feel strongly about that."

Playing like this requires discipline and an avowed adherence to your game plan. But it will usually result in far fewer dropped shots or disasters. Playing target-oriented, conditions-influenced, one-shot-at-a-time golf, the way the pros and their caddies do, is the only way to cut strokes from your score and win more consistently.

Of course, there are exceptions to every rule. At the 1992 U.S. Open, played at the famed Pebble Beach seaside course, Tom Kite, who was leading by two strokes, stepped onto the tee of the scenic but dangerous par-5 18th hole and asked his longtime caddie, Mike Carrick, "What do you think about the driver here, Mike?" Carrick was surprised: Kite had hit his 3-wood from this tee every day that week, because that had been his game plan to overcome the very tight landing area on the hole, with the seawall and Stillwater Cove lurking down the left side, and a grouping of Monterey pines and deep rough waiting for errant shots down the right side. Late on Sunday afternoon, those demanding conditions were still there, heightened by the howling wind conditions along with the tension of leading the national championship. But Carrick heard the confidence in his boss's voice and, even though, as he wrote later, "the

conditions screamed 3-wood," and he was quaking inside, he only said, "Yep, that's the club. Put a good swing on it." Carrick said the essence of being a caddie is to go with what the player is most confident in. "Sometimes you can't go by the numbers, but have to go with the feeling in a player's

Caddie Terry McNamara points the way for women's champion Annika Sorenstam.

head, hands and heart," he wrote. Tom Kite hit the driver and immediately turned to his caddie and said, "Best swing all week."

One of the conditions that every player, and his caddie, must consider in every tournament or event is the *situation* at hand. Steve Williams and Tiger Woods have a game plan for every tournament round they play. And they have a backup game plan for the last few holes. "It's very important to take a look at the last two or three holes of a tournament and decide how you're going to play them (a) if you're leading by a few, (b) if you're in a tie or one up or down, and (c) if you're behind," Williams says. "You gotta have a game plan for [each of] those situations, and when it comes to a fairly difficult hole you normally play conservatively, you're going to have to play aggressively to try and make birdies."

Tom Watson and caddie Bruce Edwards celebrate victory at the 1982 U.S. Open.

Translated to adapt to the weekend golfer, you should have planned a surefire way to make bogey on a tough closing hole, and an alternative strategy, probably a little more risky, if you have to make a par. If the situation of your match calls for the bold play, then you have the plan ready.

In summary, thinking like a caddie means you will approach all tee shots methodically. You will have a predetermined strategy for the hole based on your skills. You will select a target for the tee shot, and make it specific. You will consider all the elements, especially the wind, and choose the best club to get your ball to that target. You will then move confidently into your normal pre-shot routine and make a good swing at the ball, because you are confident in your plan, you are not trying to overswing or do the unusual, and because you have the destination — the target — in the forefront of your mind.

Piece of cake!

Think Like a Caddie, Play Like a Pro

# Checking the Caddie Checklist

Answering these essential questions will help you improve your game.

- What kind of lie do you have? Flat? Sidehill? Up or downhill? Clean in the fairway or buried in rough? Feet above or below the ball?

- Where is the wind and how strong is it? Will it knock down the ball, push it further from behind, or blow it left or right?

- What's the distance to the center of the green? What club can you hit comfortably to get the ball that distance?

- Is the pin "available?" For professionals, almost any pin is fair game— they have the knowledge and expertise to work a ball into a tucked part of the green. For weekend golfers, the best strategy is often to aim for the center of the green, or for the largest portion of the green, and hope to get down in two putts from there.

- What is the yardage needed to get over any bunkers or water hazards in front of the green?

- Where are the other no-go areas on this hole?

- Where is the safest place to land a shot? If a green is open in the front, but has all kinds of trouble waiting behind the green, then you obviously don't want to go long. Alternatively, if the front is blocked by bunkers, rough, or water, but the green is long and surrounded behind with flat grassy areas, then you want to select a club that will easily clear the front, even if it means you might go over.

## APPROACHING THE APPROACH

Let's say your tee shot made it into the fairway, reasonably close to your selected target. First, give yourself a little mental pat on the back. Nice shot! Your caddie, if you had one, would pump you up with some words of encouragement. Second, once you've hit your drive, no matter where it went, you should forget about focusing on golf until you get ready for the next shot. "You don't start talking about playing the next shot until you get near the ball," says Dean Elliott, caddie for Stephen Ames. "You can chat about other things — sports, dinner last night, whatever." Billy from Philly, who currently carries for Tim Petrovic, says that some distraction between shots is an important strategy to help the player achieve balance: "You give him other things to talk about while you walk between shots. That helps him relax and not be grinding full-time, which is a drain on energy."

Caddie Phil Morbey, a.k.a. "Wobbly," and player Jose Maria Olazabal agree on the right club.

But when you get to your ball, it's time to start thinking like a caddie. "The moment the player and caddie get to the ball, whatever they were talking about is finished and it's just full concentration that goes into the next shot that's about to be hit," says Steve Williams, in describing how he and Tiger get ready to play a shot. "Every player has a different character and a different idea when it's time to get serious."

Now you are faced with the next shot: getting the ball on the green. (We'll assume this is a par-4 hole of reasonable length — par 5s and longer 4s may call for a conservative lay up in front of the green, as the chances of finding some kind of trouble with a long-distance approach increase.)

## The Emotions of Golf

The sports psychologists who write about pro golf make it sound like you need to have your emotions on an absolutely even keel the entire day. That's not really possible and it's not what happens in a golf tournament. Hitting accurate shots and making excellent putts is going to get the player and the caddie very pumped up. To me, that's natural and it's OK to do. Look, we get excited out there. What you have to do is find a way for those emotions to go through you, and to use them for a positive energy. So yes, you can get emotional highs. Then you've got that couple of minutes between shots to even back out. You settle down, use the emotional energy in a professional way, and expect very good things from the next shot.

Actually, as a caddie, you have to keep those positive emotions flowing through you even if the round isn't going well. The way you know that you're doing that is when your player gets a very positive result from a so-so swing. The ball goes exactly where you wanted it to go and you aren't surprised, you aren't shaking your head and talking about a lucky bounce, you're juiced up because in your mind, the golf course owed you that. Your player has the talent, he makes lots of good swings that he doesn't get much out of, and now he's getting something back. So, immediately you and he are roused up and you're on the attack and you are just going to keep it up until the last putt falls in.

The one thing about getting pumped up is that eventually it will add distance to one of your shots, and both you and the player need to be ready for that. On tour it generally doesn't happen until the last hour or so on Sunday, when you're in contention. But at some point you will be at 7-iron distance and you'll have to pull that 8-iron. So you need to be smart about that.

When the round is not going well, there's a place for some anger or at least irritation. But that's just for the player. Depending on his personality type, he can get steamed up and put those feelings to use. Obviously, it's got to be controlled and under the surface. And both you and he have to know if he is ticked off at himself or if he's ticked off at the kind of results he's getting, based on the rub of the green. The caddie will react a little differently in each case.

If the player is angry with himself, you let him use the energy of it, but everything you say is positive — about how the next shot is going to be right on target. If it's anger at a bad result from a good shot, you have to make sure that doesn't feed into an overall feeling that this isn't our day. Again, the idea is that the odds are going in your favor now — and the good swings or good putts are going to have to bring good results because the law of averages is on your side.

*Bobby Brown, caddie for Dustin Johnson*

Jim Furyk reacts to one that just got away.

Once again, the important thing is to consider this shot as entirely independent and unique from every other shot you've made, either in this round, or in your life. You go through the caddie checklist (see p. 94) to gather the information you need to help you decide what club to choose for the next shot.

Considering the cold hard facts that are the answers to the questions in the checklist will help the player decide on the club that she can use with the highest degree of confidence for the shot at hand. The player must also consult her game plan, where she has noted the holes that can be played aggressively, and those that call for a conservative approach. "You have to be flexible, but you go out with a game plan," says Fred "Bassett," a longtime caddie on the Ladies European Tour. "What's the point of practice rounds if you don't make any plans? When you've got carries over bunkers or water, if it's into the wind, you don't go for it, you lay up. But if it's downwind, based on the yardage, you change your plan because you can get there in two."

Here's how Steve Williams describes the process: "When you get close to the ball, you've already got in your head a rough idea how far it is and what

Steve Williams puts "the Big Cat" back in the bag after another perfect drive by Tiger Woods.

club you're looking at. If it's an exact number [a yardage that equates to the distance Tiger likes to hit a certain club], I tell him first and he'll say, 'Yeah, I agree with that,' or 'Maybe this instead.' Whatever, it's obviously not going to be more than one club off, either way.

"I give him the yardage and tell him what I think the club is and wait for him to come back to me. Ninety percent of caddies do it the other way around, where the caddie gives the information and the player pulls what he thinks is the right club. I tell them what I think up front and that gives the player a starting point. I don't think he needs a lot of information but some players need more information than others. I caddy more by feel and by knowing my player and what he likes to do. There are times when you see a different opinion on a shot, but most of the time you know what sort of shot they're going to play. You know how he plays his wedges; you know what he likes to do, and what he doesn't like to do. You don't have to ask. It's just instinct."

Watch the team of caddie and player work on television on any of the tours. Note the process of deciding on a club. The player approaches the ball and checks out his lie. The caddie comes up and gives him the yardage and the wind and, sometimes, suggests a club. The player absorbs this data while he is studying the shot, choosing his target and deciding how to work the ball to that spot. Finally . . . the last thing he does . . . is pull a club. Then he goes into his pre-shot routine and makes the shot.

Far too often, weekend golfers do it backwards. They come up to their ball, note the yardage, and pull a club. Then they have to mentally justify that decision, which usually means ignoring the objective evidence right in front of them.

Once you've pulled the club, it's imperative to choose the target again, just like you did from the tee. Again, you need to zero in on a specific target, not something generic like "the green." If you're shooting for the pin, that's obviously a good target to have in your mind. But if you're shooting for the middle of the green, then, again, select some kind of mark on the ground as your target — the more specific you can make the target, the better your mind will respond by producing the right shot to get there.

Finally, based on the data, the club selected for a shot should be the one that will allow the easiest swing. Let's say you have an approach shot of 150 yards to a green with bunkers in front. Your analysis of the elements tells you that there's a slight wind in your face, and the pin is cut five yards back from the center of the green. Normally, you choose your 7-iron for all shots from 150 yards. But for this shot, you know you don't want to land in that front bunker, you know the pin is

back, and you know the wind is slightly hurting. You could still use your 7-iron, but you'd have to step on it to avoid that front bunker and get the ball all the way back to the pin. Thinking like a caddie, you instead choose a 6-iron and make a nice, relaxed, three-quarter power swing, letting the club do all the hard work of flying the ball over the bunker and getting it back to the pin. Even if you don't hit it perfectly, which as a weekend golfer is always a good possibility, the 6-iron provides you with the best chance to at least fly that front bunker and get the ball somewhere on the green.

That's how professional players and caddies approach their approach shots: choosing the easiest club they can hit to get the ball where they want it to go. The best results happen when one swings effortlessly, in control and in balance. Making a shot with three-quarters effort, rather than swinging out of your shoes, almost always results in a better, more accurate, and more solidly struck golf shot.

This same philosophy is the guiding principle on par-5 holes, where the weekend golfer often hits the driver from the tee and the 3-wood from the fairway without first thinking through a strategy for the hole. Golf pros make their money by reaching par-5 holes in two long shots, putting for eagles and birdies. For the rest of us, making a par should be no problem if we have a plan to make three easy shots to get the ball on the green, allowing two putts for five. Why try to hit the ball as far as possible with the first two shots, which often leads to trouble?

Your strategy for most par-5 holes should be the simplest one. Play the hole backwards in your mind. From what distance do you have the best accuracy hitting into a green? From 120 yards with a 9-iron? From 100 yards with a pitching wedge? From seventy-five yards with a sand wedge? Select that "mayor's office" location first, and figure out how to get the ball there with your first two shots. You might just need an easy 3-wood from the tee, a relaxed

4- or 5-iron down the fairway and bingo, you're in the office, chatting with His Excellency!

Thinking like a caddie means eliminating all ego, all former history, all expectation of hitting a perfect shot, and concentrating instead on simply playing the game one shot at a time. Each shot, is a different adventure and presents a different challenge to be solved. When you think like a caddie, you devise the easiest solution to each challenge, which, in turn, allows you to play each shot with confidence, knowing that each shot has been well thought out and is the perfect one for you to play.

## TROUBLE SHOTS: NEVER MAKE IT WORSE

Now let's assume that something has gone wrong and your shot ends up in trouble. It happens . . . this is golf, after all. As that famous Scotsman, Robert Burns, once wrote: "The best laid schemes o' mice an' men gang aft agley," which, roughly translated, means: "Everyone makes mistakes in golf."

Nobody — neither trained professionals nor weekend hackers — enjoys screwing up a shot. It's not like any of us tries to send a shot sailing into the woods or the rough or the bunkers . . . it just happens. Part of the game.

The secret for scoring in such situations is to never make a bad situation worse. Eli Brown has been caddying at Seminole Golf Club in Florida for both accomplished golfers and weekend hackers. He's seen more bad shots than any one of us will make in a lifetime! What does he say to his player after a bad shot? "If you hit a bad shot, let's go to the next shot and have some patience," he will say. "And do the right thing here, be patient and trust in your swing. And get back on course."

That's one of the beauties of playing golf one shot at a time. If you hit a bad one, you can forget it and move on to the most important shot . . . the next one. That's easy to conceptualize and hard to do in reality. It is so easy to get down in golf, to become angry at ourselves and self-berating over our failures. And because most of us are weekend golfers, those failures are frequent and alarmingly familiar.

But being angry and down isn't going to get the ball into the hole in the fewest number of strokes. Playing with relaxed confidence will. So after a bad shot,

## How Caddies Make Decisions About Selecting the Right Club

you've got to process the bad emotions and then let them go. If you must, give yourself thirty seconds to moan and groan, tell yourself what a dummy you are, you've made that shot a hundred times before, how could you do what you just did, etc., etc., etc. Then, forget it and move on to examine the next shot.

Sports psychologists and golf caddies are a lot alike, in that they earn their money by helping athletes live in the moment, turn away from negative thoughts, stay focused on the objective (hitting the next shot to the next target), and think about the process of hitting a good shot while remaining disassociated from the results. One guru tells his students to think, after a shot goes awry, "Well, that was certainly interesting." In that way, there is no assigning blame, or any kind of self-abasement for the failure of the shot — it just happened and it is interesting to make an objective observation of it.

Caddies are always trying to eliminate negative thoughts and keep their players thinking of the next shot, not the last one. "You've gotta put bad stuff behind you," says Steve Williams, whose player, Tiger Woods, is rarely in that position. "You gotta continue when things don't go well, but put them behind you. You've got to be positive, always, and that's the really hard thing. We all know one goes through bad patches, but you've always got to remain positive so you can turn things around."

So, once you've hit a bad shot and given yourself thirty seconds to think about it, put it out of

We start off obviously with the yardage, then we look for trouble areas; [we determine] where would be best and what we should steer away from. . . . Basically, as soon as I get a [yardage] number I'll know pretty much [that] it's gonna be one of two clubs . . .
and then I start thinking about why one club would be better than the other and . . . we talk all the way through about each shot . . . [The player] will ask me questions, and . . . I'll ask her questions. . . . I give the facts and then I can always tell if she's happy or unhappy with my suggestions and she'll make a suggestion.

We talk about how far it's actually playing. . . . We've got a yardage 150, then we take hill (if it's uphill/downhill) and wind into account. This 150 yardage could be playing 162. Then we have to work out where we have to land it if the greens are releasing. I'll never say to her what club I think it is; I'll tell her what I think the yardage is . . . and then she'll suggest a club to me . . . or she'll ask, "What do you think?" I would never say what club to hit.

Ultimately, I have to make her realize that what she's about to do is absolutely 100 percent correct . . . . If there is a little bit of doubt in my mind, I have to make her believe it's absolutely right, as she can't go into a shot thinking, "This maybe isn't right," and I'd rather a player put a good swing on it . . . and end up being slightly wrong, than put a bad swing on it when it could have been right. . . . You have [to] get them completely confident walking into a shot.

Mike Patterson,
*caddie for Karrie Webb, Joanne Morley,*
*Janice Moodie, and Mhairi McKay*

> "The only time I talk on the golf course is to my caddie. And then [it's] only to complain when he gives me the wrong club."
> — Severiano Ballesteros, world #1 golfer

your mind and begin thinking about the next shot. When you find yourself in trouble — deep in the woods or the rough, or just generally out of position or off your game plan for a hole — the first consideration should always be "How can I get back onto the course and back into play?" Trying to make up for one bad shot by trying something miraculous with the next one is usually a recipe for disaster.

It all goes back to knowing your capabilities and not trying to exceed them. Whether trying to hit a driver 325 yards, a 9-iron 150 yards, or keep a low screaming hook underneath the branches of a tree so the ball will roll onto the green, the weekend golfer is likely to come up short simply because he lacks the skill and experience needed to pull off those kinds of shots. The professional golfer, who has years of experience behind her and has likely practiced all kinds of recovery shots, is much more likely to have success with difficult recovery shots. The late Bob Rosburg was always chided for his television commentary when he'd say, "Johnny, he's got no shot . . . no shot at all." Most of the time, the pro in question not only *had* a shot, he quite often made it onto the green. They know how to do stuff like that — we don't.

One caddie once worked for Corey Pavin, the U.S. Open winner in 1995, and during one tournament followed him and an errant shot into the woods. "I was convinced that he'd have to chip the ball out sideways to get it back onto the fairway," the caddie recalls. "I mean, he barely had room to swing the club unimpeded by the branches, and the route to the green seemed to me to be totally blocked by tree trunks and thick-growing branches and bushes. But he pulled out a club and punched it through all the garbage and the ball ran onto and just off the back of the green. That's when I realized that pro golfers are different from the rest of us."

We can admire and appreciate that kind of acumen on a golf course, but trying to do the same thing ourselves just results in triple-bogies and worse. It is far better strategy to simply choose the easiest way back onto the fairway and play on from there. Matt Achatz, Rocco Mediate's caddie, likes to think after his man hits a bad shot: "Where do I have to hit the ball so we can still make par?" Weekend golfers should think: "Where do I have to hit my ball to get back in play to continue this hole without losing any more shots?"

As with any other shot, you must approach a recovery shot with the same objective mindset. First, examine the situation of the shot: Do I have a swing? A good lie? An opening back to the course? Next, think about the options. Do I have to hit it low to keep it under branches? Do I need extra loft to get out of deep rough? How will the ball react? Finally, select the target and choose the club that will best and most easily get the ball there.

Then, forget about it and move on.

Every shot you play, from first tee to the last putt on 18, must be approached in this way. Each shot presents its own challenge and opportunity and each one must be taken by itself and solved. If you can play eighteen holes that way, your scores will drop like a rock.

## GOING MENTAL: SECRETS OF POSITIVE THINKING

Every caddie from Steve Williams on down knows that he is not going to have a good payday if his player is not playing with confidence. "It's 100 percent important," Steve says. "There's no point in a player standing over a shot if [he's] not confident."

Every golfer has probably had the experience of playing well, for a round, for a portion of a round, maybe just for a shot or two in a row. They know the feeling of getting ready to hit a shot knowing, in their heart of hearts, that it's going to be a good one. The sports psychologists call it being "in the zone," and make a lot of money trying to tell the rest of us how to get there.

Pros and caddies know about the zone, and they also know how to get themselves into that head space, at least for the short time it takes to hit a golf ball. The entire process discussed in this chapter, the one-shot-at-a-time attitude, the careful collection of information about a shot, and the choice of the best and easiest option are the ways they go about getting there. With a target in mind, based on an intelligent review of the facts concerning the shot, the player can go ahead and produce a good shot to get the ball to that target. Then they relax as they stroll up the fairway to the next shot, thinking about dinner or sports or anything *but* golf until they reach the ball. They play with relaxed confidence, relying on their abilities and experience to deliver good results. When things go badly, as they do from time to time, they don't try harder, *they try less hard*.

Caddies keep an eye on their player, and know when to nudge him back into this state of relaxed concentration. Rocco Mediate says his caddie, Matt Achatz, occasionally tells him to slow down. Achatz notices when he is walking too fast or swinging too fast. "Of course, when we get behind a slow group and I start to complain, he'll say, 'What do you want to do, wait on this guy or go hang shingles on a roof?' He's right, of course."

Some players — but a very few — can actually play better when they're angry. Rory Sabbatini is one, according to his caddie, Kevin Fasbender. "Rory is one of those rare players who can get angry and use it to his advantage. Sometimes anger helps put him right in 'the zone,' as they say. But he's not typical that way, so if a player can't get angry and channel it pretty naturally, the caddie is responsible for helping cool him down."

Mike Carrick, longtime caddie for Tom Kite, speaks of stepping into "the bubble," a place where Kite feels confident and strong. "Most players and caddies try very hard to create a sedate 'bubble' of calmness around them when competing in a tournament," Carrick writes in his book *Caddie Sense*. "My job . . . is to eliminate as many confidence-sapping situations as possible so that he can be clear of mind. . . . Bad thoughts are like viruses . . . they multiply until the host is incapacitated."

Have you ever gone an entire round without adding up your score before you've finished? Have you ever completely forgotten about score and concentrated only on making shots one at a time? It's very hard to do, but it can be incredibly liberating for your game if you're able to forget the results and just concentrate on the process. In the final singles round of the 2009 President's Cup matches, played at San Francisco's Harding Park, Tiger Woods was playing against Y.E. Yang, and eventually closed him out, 6 and 5. He was then told by the TV announcer walking with his group that his point had clinched the Cup. "Really?" Tiger said, amazed. "I wasn't paying attention to the score. I just wanted to win my match, so I kept my head down and plowed on."

There will be plenty of time after the round to count up the strokes and evaluate the results. While you're playing, you should only be thinking one shot at a time.

Tiger and Steve focusing on the task at hand: to think about the next shot and nothing else.

# Chapter 7
## Mastering the Greens

"If I were water, where would I go?"

— *Bradley S. Klein,*
*architecture editor of* Golfweek *and former caddie*

# 7

## Mastering the Greens

If the old mantra "drive for show, putt for dough" is true, then caddies — and those who think like caddies — really earn their keep when the game arrives at the green. After all, the physical act of putting a golf ball does not require brute strength. But getting the ball into the hole demands a close reading of the elements and some savvy decision-making. That's what caddies do best.

Give a small child a putter and a ball and tell them the point of the game is to hit the ball into that hole over there, and they will quickly understand the problem. First, they'll whack the ball too hard and then, overcompensating, too meekly. Lesson: to get the ball to fall into the hole, it must be traveling at the right speed — fast enough to get to the hole, but not so fast as to go careening across the green. Then, they'll see that because the green is tilted and rolling, uphill and down, they need to get the ball rolling in the correct direction, so that the undulations and topography of the putting surface will turn the ball towards the hole.

That's pretty much it. Within a minute or two, most kids would be happily stroking putts with ease, laughing with glee when the ball goes in, and giggling at the silliness of it all when the ball just misses. As long as you don't tell them

Annika gets a read from her caddie, Terry McNamara, as she lines up a putt on the 5th green during the second round of the July 2000 U.S. Women's Open Championship

Analyzing the data: Andrew Magee and caddie Eric Meller look over a putt.

that making or missing a putt has serious consequences — like winning or losing the Masters or the club championship — it will all be just a fun game out in the sunshine with a ball and a stick.

Some think reading greens is an art, others consider it a science. Caddies look at it as just another shot, and approach it the same way they do a tee shot or an approach. They work with the player to gather the information, decide on a course of action, focus on the target, and proceed with confidence. Distill putting down to its essence — the balance between speed and line — and it's pretty simple. It's only the subjective weight of the results of the putt (good for make, bad for miss) which complicates the matter.

Caddies tend to fall into the "science" camp when it comes to reading greens. Architecture editor of *Golfweek* and former caddie Bradley S. Klein boils green-reading down to one simple thought: "If I were water, where would I go?"

But mastering the greens on a particular golf course begins well before the round of golf is played. One of the first things a caddie will ascertain about a golf course is the lay of the land. In Palm Springs, they ask "Which way is Indio?" because that town sits at the lowest part of the Coachella Valley, and like water, putts tend to fall towards the lowest point. On mountain courses, the highest peak is often noted, as the terrain and putts will often veer away from it. On courses built near a collecting body of water — a river, a lake, or the ocean — the same principle applies: the direction in which water flows is often the direction in which putts will turn.

Caddies take note of these macro-conditions even as they begin to gather the data around each green. Architects may design greens with all kinds of humps and mounds, undulations and ridges, but every green has an underlying and basic orientation, a high and a low point. "Find the high side of the green first," Klein advises. "Then note the subordinate slopes. Your best bet is to stand behind the green to see which way it slants overall."

In essence, caddies read a green three different ways, from wide-angle to tight focus:

- The orientation of the golf course; namely, the surrounding terrain.

- The orientation of the green to the golf course.

- The orientation of the ball to the green.

Those who read putts only by considering the terrain between the ball and the hole are often fated to miss many of them. Remember, every shot is unique unto itself and must be considered on its own merits, even on the green. That means paying attention to terrain and other elements that may affect the shot, even a short putt.

As we discussed in previous chapters, the wind can affect a putt. Caddies know that if the wind is strong enough to straighten out the flag atop the pin or make one's pants legs flap, it is strong enough to blow a putt offline, slow one heading into the wind, or speed up one travelling downwind. They note these conditions and will mention them to their player.

Time of day also has an affect on a putt. In the mornings, when there is still some dew on the grass, putts will often be slower than they look. Conversely, as the day wears on and the sun beats down, greens can get slicker and faster. Add the drying effects of a stiff breeze, and they can get faster still. Late in the afternoon, after a full day in the hot sun, the blades of grass on a putting green will grow, and on *Poa annua* grass greens, the plants will put out tiny blooms. All of that can affect the grain of the green and the speed of putts.

Speaking of grain, that is another important consideration for anyone "reading" greens. Bent-grass greens, found mainly in the northern tier of states, have a subtle grain which tends to follow the direction of draining water. *"If you were water, where would you go?"* That's where the grain will go as well.

## The Overnight Putt

Caddies are often asked to help read putts for their players. But rarely are they asked to wait all night to see if their read is correct.

Damon Green was on Scott Hoch's bag at the 2003 Ford Championship at the Doral Resort in Miami. Green had played a few years on the Nike Tour and just missed earning his card to play on the PGA Tour in Q-School. He already had one win on Hoch's bag when they came into Miami and ended up tied with Jim Furyk at the end of regulation play. The two began a playoff.

They tied on the first playoff hole, the 18th at Doral's Blue Monster course, and headed for the 1st hole. The sun was sinking rapidly into the Everglades as they played the par-5 hole. It got darker as the two players finally arrived on the green, Hoch with a seven-footer for birdie, Furyk with a makeable four-footer for his bird.

Green and Hoch both read the putt and compared notes. "We read the putt as it was getting kinda dark," Green recalled later. "Scott asked me and I told him it was left edge. He said 'Really? I think it's right edge!'"

Under the Rules of Golf, a player can decide if the conditions — in this case, darkness — make it impossible to continue play. Hoch had had Lasik surgery, with some complications afterwards, and the growing darkness made his depth perception fuzzy. So he requested the tournament be postponed until the next morning. The television producers and the assembled fans groaned, but the rules were clear.

"I stayed up all night wondering how he could have gotten right edge when I had it left edge!" Green stated later. "The grain, everything was going to the right."

In the morning, before warming up, Hoch asked his caddie to go out to the 1st green and look at the putt again. Green first found a tournament official and checked to make sure he was allowed to go out and survey the putt before play began. He was, he did, and came back to report it was still left edge. "So we practiced left-edge putts on the putting green before we went out and when we got to the green, Scott looked at the putt again and told me I was correct. He knocked it in, Jim made his, and we went to the next hole."

Hoch birdied the third playoff hole to win.

Damon Green and Scott Hoch had to sleep on an important read.

Bermuda-grass greens, usually found in the hot and humid parts of the country, have a distinct graining characteristic. For the most part, Bermuda grain tends to grow in the direction of the setting sun. Those who play mainly on such greens know that one can usually tell by the color of the grass which way the grain is heading. If the grass has a deeper shade of green, it usually means you're looking into the grain; a down-grain section of the green will have a lighter, almost waxy appearance. The more upright growing characteristic of Bermuda grass means that the grain will have a great affect on a putted golf ball — it will slow down all putts hit into the grain, and make down-grain putts faster.

When professional caddies are making up their yardage books, they will spend a lot of time examining each green to determine how each of these factors might affect a putted ball. A pro's book will usually have a dot indicating the high point nearest the green, and some arrows showing the direction of the grain and the slopes. Once the player and his caddie arrive at the green, they will then assess the other elements before zeroing in on the putt itself. Sometimes, that analysis starts before the player gets onto the green: Bruce Edwards said that his boss, Tom Watson, would begin to read a green from thirty yards away as he walked up the fairway. From a distance, he could see the orientation and overall slope of the green; once he got close he could then observe the other important factors involved in the upcoming shot.

Bruce Edwards and Tom Watson doing their thing on the green.

## Tiger's Putting Routine

As with any other golf stroke, successful putting requires a repeatable routine for preparing to make a shot. The world's best golfer, Tiger Woods, has his putting routine down, and it's one the rest of us would do well to emulate.

Like many pro golfers, Woods marks his ball with a straight line on the equator, which he uses as an alignment guide in setting up his putt. When he's getting ready to putt, Tiger will use that line to point where he thinks he wants to aim. He'll leave his ball marker on the green while he makes up his mind.

He usually walks to the hole to examine areas where the ball may change direction or where the grain intercedes on the line. Walking behind the hole, he will look back at his ball while he thinks about distance and elevation.

Returning to his marked ball, he will then make a minute adjustment to line up his aiming line with the line on the ball. When he's satisfied, he'll pick up the marker.

Then he goes behind the ball, crouches, places his hands on either side of the bill of his cap to shut out any visual distractions, and makes a final check of his line. It's very likely that he also visualizes his putt rolling down the line and into the hole.

Stepping up to the ball, Tiger places the putter, also known as the blade, behind the ball with his right hand and then places his feet to align with the blade. He'll take two practice swings without stopping, and then make a final look at the hole — his target. Rotating his head back to look down at the ball, he'll settle his feet, rotate his head for one more look, rotate back to the ball, focus, and swing.

The entire process takes about a minute. The results speak for themselves.

### WHAT'S MY LINE?

Once the macro factors have been assimilated, you can begin to zero in on your specific putt. While there are no hard and fast rules, most golfers will "see" the line of a putt first, before they think about speed. The line, of course, is the path the ball will take to get to the hole. The terrain of the putting surface is a major consideration in determining which way the ball will break and by how much.

Tiger follows the same routine for all his putts.

One of the universal indications that a golfer is a weekend player is that he constantly under-reads putts. At the golf schools run by short-game guru Dave Pelz, students are asked to estimate the break on an innocent-looking putt the instructors will set up. Most guesses from the class will range from twelve inches to about three feet. The correct answer is usually double or triple the widest estimate. Pelz actually recommends tripling the amount of break you see in a putt and then aiming there.

A putt that misses the hole on the high side of the break is usually called "missing on the pro side" because professionals always read more break into a putt than the weekend hacker. They also know that over-reading the break is much better than the opposite, as a putt on the high side always has a chance of turning and falling into the hole, whereas once a ball breaks below the hole, it isn't ever going to roll back uphill and into the cup!

Putting is a constant exercise in observation and adjustment. On the 1st hole, you hit your putt based on your best guess of how the ball will react to the terrain and conditions, and then watch what happens. If the result is good, you continue doing that. If it's not so good, you adjust your thinking for the next putt. So if your putts are consistently missing on the low side, you should take note and start to aim a bit higher on your putts from that point on.

When working on divining the correct line, it's important to look at a putt from every angle — again, without unduly holding up play. Trying to make a putt based only on the perspective you have standing behind the ball is a one-dimensional exercise in futility. The pros and their caddies will walk all around a putt — the full 360 degrees — in order to pick up any subtle slopes. They will also find the fall line of the main slope and use that to judge the amount of break on the angle their putt will travel. Note that they do most of that walking around before it's their turn to putt, which helps speed up play.

It is also imperative to pay attention to your playing partners' putts as well, even if their putting line is nowhere near similar to your own. You can get a lot of good information on the speed of the greens by watching another putt or two; and you will see how the putt reacts as it gets close to the hole. That's information that will be helpful to your own efforts.

## SPEED TRAPS

If choosing the correct line is most important, hitting the putt at the right speed is a close second. After all, the speed with which you hit a putt helps determine how much break the ball will take on the green: the harder you hit the ball the straighter it rolls; and as the ball begins to slow down, it is more affected by the slopes and slants in the green. A "lag putt" usually involves a long putt over varied terrain and is one that attempts to get the ball close enough to the hole for an easy second putt, hopefully a "tap-in."

Caddies on the pro tours know that most of the players like to be aggressive on the greens. For the pros, birdies equate to money. And, because they practice putting by the hour, they are not worried about making those frustrating three-foot comebackers. Joe Pyland, the current looper for Boo Weekley, says, "If you are an amateur golfer, try and change your mindset about medium-to-long approach putts. Especially the moderately straight ones. All the amateurs I see stand over these putts thinking about speed in a totally defensive way. They are really just lagging randomly, toward a semi-circle that is left, short, and right of the hole. They need to start with the line, commit to the line, and pick a speed that truly gives the putt a chance to go in. If it goes by five feet and everybody groans, don't listen to them, 'cause they're all just scared laggers themselves!"

Although one must always choose the right time, committing to putting aggressively will result in more made putts than trying to lag everything close. The great philosopher Yogi Berra is credited with the sage saying that "Ninety percent of short putts don't go in," leaving the rest of us to wonder about the other 10 percent of short putts! Yogi notwithstanding, it should be obvious that a putt must be hit hard enough to reach the hole to have any chance of going in.

Tiger Woods is just the leading example of an aggressive putter, especially on those knee-knocking five-footers. While weekend golfers will try to steer those shorter putts into the cup, Woods steps up and rams them home, taking out most of the break on those putts with a firm speed. He rarely misses, of course, but even when he does, he knows he can usually make the return putt, even if it's another five-footer.

Whenever a caddie begins working with a new player, one of the first and most important things he has to learn is what kind of putter the player is. Some pros like to putt at what is called "cup speed;" they try to die the ball into the hole

Any which way: Mickelson tries the cross-footed stroke on the practice green.

on its last revolution. Others, like Woods, prefer to maintain some pace on the ball as it reaches the hole, so it does have enough speed to reach and roll past the hole. Dave Pelz, the short-game guru who has done exhaustive studies and research into putting, recommends as the optimum speed one that will carry the ball eighteen inches past the hole. Woody Austin's caddie, Brent Henley, explains: "The best caddie in the world is not going to be able to give a player good reads right away if he doesn't know the player. You've got to figure out whether the golfer wants a 'cup speed' read or a read for a putt that is going to get to the hole with some pace left over. If the player is always hitting firm putts, the caddie will have to read the line according to that."

The major factors in putting speed, in addition to the power of the stroke, are the slope, the grain, and sometimes the wind. As the player is lining up his putt, those are the elements that he must consider.

Finally, success in putting comes when the player treats a putt like any other golf shot. After the survey of conditions, the selection of the line, and the calculation of the speed, the golfer should choose an aiming point . . . the target. Obviously, the target is the hole. But as a target, "the hole" is much too generic. Just as "the green" is not specific enough as a target for an approach shot, the target on the green must be narrowed down to a much tighter focus.

For a straight putt, the target should be a very specific part of the hole. Find a tuft of grass or a discoloration on the edge of the center of the hole and make that tiny spot the target — try to roll the ball over that selected tuft of grass.

For a breaking putt, the target may not be anywhere near the hole, but a point on the line where you want the putt to start out. Choose some kind of mark on the green and focus only on getting the ball rolling toward that spot. If you've chosen the right line and hit the ball with the right speed, the ball that starts out on line towards that target will take the break and curve towards the hole, just as you've imagined.

"I was lying ten and had a thirty-five-foot putt. I whispered over my shoulder: 'How does this one break?' And my caddie said, 'Who cares?'"
— actor Jack Lemmon

In addition to choosing and putting at a target, the player must remember that a putt is still a golf stroke that must be performed with rhythm and timing. Tiger Woods is always talking about "releasing the putter" when he speaks of his greenside game. What he means is that he wants to make a full stroke with the putter, without decelerating, pushing, or pulling with the hands. When he can make a nice, smooth, and complete putting stroke, all the way back and all the way through, he knows he will have better results. You will too.

Waiting their turn: Michelle Wie and caddie-dad B.J. on the tee.

# Chapter 8

## Count 'Em Up

"You need benchmarks for your basic skills. Assessing performance from tee to green and in the short game — with real numbers that you write down and review — would be extremely beneficial for any player who wants to bring out his best in competition."

— Mike Granuzzo,
founder and president, Caddie Master Enterprises

# 8

## Count 'Em Up:
## How the Stats Can Work for You

On the PGA Tour's Web site, you can find up-to-the-minute statistics in thirty-one different categories of play for each player, ranging from his or her final-round scoring average, to driving accurary, to sand saves, to "bounce back" (the percent of time a player is over par on a hole and under par on the next hole).

For the most part, these figures exist mainly for the pleasure of fantasy-golf team owners and stats nerds. According to most tour caddies, players will occasionally glance at their statistics, perhaps to confirm a suspicion, say, that their sand play hasn't been as sharp recently as they'd like, but they don't do a lot of introspective stat-gazing.

"When people think about tour players using stats, they usually mean the stats you see on the PGA Tour website — fairways hit, greens in regulation," says Brett Waldman, looper for Camilo Villegas. "We pay attention to that, but a lot of the time you keep your own stats that are a little more specific to your own game's needs."

It's in the book: Paul Azinger's caddie explains the options for the next shot.

Statistics are only useful when they can be applied to your game and used in helping you find areas of weakness that need attention. For the weekend golfer, then, tracking the number of 3-putt greens would be far more informative than knowing what one's average driving distance was.

Waldman has some suggestions on the kinds of statistics that might be more useful to the weekend golfer: "One place that the amateur golfer might start is by keeping a stat on putts he leaves right of the hole and those that go left of the hole. Not so much the big breaking putts but the makeable putts with a normal amount of break — a cup or so. The tendency is to keep missing on one side or the other." Knowing that you are missing a lot of straight five-footers on the right side tells you a great deal: about alignment, about speed and maybe even about how you're reading greens.

Just as the savvy golfer should construct his own yardage book to his own golfing specifications and abilities, he should begin to keep track of important statistics for his own game. Over just a short amount of time, say after four or five rounds, one's personal golf statistics can reveal some amazing truths.

Freddie Couples and caddie Joe LaCava at the 2006 Open Championship.

Collecting one's personal statistics is easy enough. You can use a separate notebook, make notations in your yardage book or, the easiest of all, pick up a blank scorecard and use the boxes where the score goes to enter your stats. You can use shorthand, such as "F" for fairway in regulation, "G" for green in regulation, and small dots to indicate number of putts. Once you get home, you can enter your stats into a spreadsheet program or just write them down in a journal or notebook.

Here are some of the potential categories for data collection:

It's another GIR (green in regulation) for Rich Beem and his caddie, Billy Heim.

**From the tee:**

**Fairways hit.** It's always a good thing to hit your tee ball into the fairway. Be sure and note which club you used for each tee shot. This may show you which of your longer clubs — driver vs. 3-wood — is the more accurate, an important piece of data to have when the situation gets particularly tense during the closing holes of a match.

**Shot direction.** Maybe you say you have no idea where your tee shot is going! Track a few rounds and the numbers will tell you whether your tendency is to hit a hook or a fade, a pull or a push, a high pop-up or a low runner. You'll also be able to track where your shot goes on certain difficult holes: you may notice, for instance, that you always slice a drive on a difficult hole, indicating that tension or stress is causing you to open up on those shots.

**Pro stat to ignore:** driving distance. You don't care how far down the fairway you can launch a golf ball. You care about how close you can get your tee shot to your selected target on each hole, whether that target is 175 yards away or 225 yards away.

The numbers game: statistics can tell one a lot about the state of his or her game.

From the fairway

**Greens hit per plan.** The pros want to know how many "greens in regulation" they hit — meaning how many times they reach a par 4 with the second or approach shot; or a par 5 with the third shot. Your personal strategy ignores all that and instead outlines the plan you have devised for each hole based on your skill. So you may have planned to reach the green on a difficult par-4 hole with your third shot, a short wedge or chip. If so, you should mark that hole as one where you hit the green per your plan.

**Misses per club.** As part of your ongoing assessment of your golfing skills, you should make a note on each shot: did you hit your target or miss? In which direction did you miss, left or right, short or long? After collecting this data, you may begin to discern patterns — a lot of misses with the 4-iron, for instance — or a noticeable trend, such as missing to the left with almost every 7-iron shot. Collecting this data will help you focus your practice plans better, and may indicate a need to have a professional club fitter take a look at some of your clubs to see if something is out of plumb.

**Bunker escapes.** Tracking sand-saves is an exercise in frustration for weekend golfers. Most of us don't get the ball up-and-down from the sand enough times to count on one hand! More meaningful for weekend golfers are the following points: How many times can you get out of a bunker on the first try? How far from the hole do your bunker shots land? Do your shots land left or right of the target? This kind of data allows you to practice more, to modify your stance in a bunker, or to determine if your game plan needs to be adjusted to keep you away from bunkers at all costs.

**Trouble escapes.** Likewise, track the number of shots you need to get yourself out of trouble and back in position. You should see a direct correlation between one-shot escapes and lower scores on those holes.

Around the greens

**Short shots.** The pros are concerned about getting up and down from off the green, eliminating bogies or worse. Weekend golfers should focus on how close their short shots get them to the target. Begin by tracking

## Stats and Practice: Get a Baseline for Performance

Phil Mickelson showed golf fans some heavy-duty practice discipline with the "clock drill" he developed for honing his technique on short putts. Several times a week for many years, Mickelson has found a quiet corner of the putting green and forced himself to hole ten sets of ten three-foot putts in a row from all around the hole — miss at any point in the drill and he dutifully starts over.

Well, when that drill is successfully complete, Phil the Thrill can tell you categorically how many consecutive three-footers he is able to hole. It's a fine and valuable thing to keep stats on how you perform during a regulation round of golf, but savvy caddies as well as tour stars like Mickelson also point out the importance of stat-keeping during practice.

Making a tally of how reliably you can two-putt on a flat practice green from thirty feet, or how many wedges out of ten will hit the closest, largest target green on your club's range is valuable, according to Mike Granuzzo, founder and president of Caddie Master Enterprises, a company that staffs and manages caddie programs at resorts and clubs around the country. "You need benchmarks for your basic skills," says Granuzzo. "Assessing performance from tee to green and in the short game — with real numbers that you write down and review — would be extremely beneficial for any player who wants to bring out his best in competition." If you compete in club tournaments throughout the year, Granuzzo suggests a skills check like this every few months.

One reason to test and score yourself like this in practice is that you're relaxed and free of any pressure. As you get used to conducting the self-check, you could graduate to a regimen that is more like what sports psychologist Glen Albaugh emphasizes — deliberately adding tournament pressure to the process. Citing research published in a Swedish journal of psychology, Albaugh says it's a proven fact that replicating competitive situations in practice makes the on-range work carry over to the course much more efficiently. To follow his advice, repeat the skills test you did on the range and practice green, this time picking a golf course you know well and visualizing each test shot having to hit a fairway, green, or layup landing area on that course. Do the same for the greenside shots and putts you are measuring.

If you perform both versions of these tests, you'll be able to see where your basic skill weaknesses are and, at a later stage, see which of those skills hold up well under pressure and which do not.

— *David Gould*

Annika Sorenstam and her sister Charlotta Sorenstam line up putts on the 5th hole during the practice round of the 2002 U.S. Women's Open at the Cherry Hills Country Club in Denver, Colorado.

how many chips and pitches during a round finish within ten feet of the hole, a reasonable result for a high-handicap golfer. A second stat could be shots that finish within five feet. The golfer who can get most of his short shots to finish close to the hole will begin to see his scores drop like a rock.

Make some notes about the different clubs used for these shots as well. You may find that hitting some chips and pitches with low-irons instead of a lofted sand wedge every time may yield some better results.

There is also a lot of information you can collect about yourself on the greens themselves:

**Number of 3-putts**. It may be ugly and depressing, but you should know how many times a round you 3-jack it (or worse!). Write it down, learn the truth, and then do something about it: either hit your approach shots closer to the hole or practice your lag and long-distance putting more.

**Misses.** Do you miss the hole more on the left or on the right? How many putts do you leave short? How many putts do you charge past the hole and miss coming back? Everybody has bad putting days, but if the data begin to show trends, its time to do something about it.

**Three-footers.** These should be your "money" putts, the distance from which you make more than you miss, especially in important matches and situations. Note your percentage of makes vs. misses.

### Overall game stats

Your personal statistics book should also contain some data that tell you what you need to know for your game and game plan.

For instance, we've recommended that thinking like a caddie means choosing a target for every shot, and using the available data at hand to select a club to hit the ball to that target. You might want to track something like "targets hit" among your personal stats, to let you know how successful you are in playing to your plan. If you find your percentage of hits is lower than you'd like, you should think about reworking the plan to make it easier to hit a target.

Write down a list of all "good shots made." At first, this list may be very light — maybe just four or five good shots per round. But as you keep track of them, noting the situation, the club you used, the elements involved in the shot, and the decision-making that went into those shots, you will begin to see improvement on the rest of your shots.

Sports psychologists always point out that weekend golfers know instantly why a shot turned out badly. As soon as the ball leaves the club, we exclaim, "Oh, I hit that one thin" or "Nope, lifted my head," or some other self-diagnosis that is usually spot-on. But rarely do we hit an almost perfect shot and say, "Wow, I shifted my weight perfectly on that one!" or "Man oh man, was my timing good then!"

Spend a few minutes after a round of golf to remember the good shots, even if there were just a few. Don't forget to remember the good putts, too, either the lag putt that results in a tap-in, or a nice five-footer that helped you win a hole when the pressure was on.

Do you do the same thing for bad shots? Do you write down all your "failures" in stark black and white? If you say no . . . remember, bad shots are "interesting" and nothing more. But when you review a round of golf, you should review the decision-making that went into *each* shot, not just the results. If, for instance, you dumped an easy iron-shot into the lake, you should review and remember the process that led to that shot, not the shot itself. Did you step up to that shot with full confidence that you had the right club for the right shot? Were you uncomfortable about the stance? The lie? Was it a pressure situation in the match? Or was it your game plan that was at fault? Did you really need to hit that shot across the water, or was there an easier, alternate route that might have been taken?

Almost every player-caddie pair on the pro tour spends some time reviewing the round that they just completed, and goes over the shots, good and bad, that contributed to the day's score. "After a round you summarize how the day went, where you did particularly well, [or where] you had trouble with this hole, whether we can work it out on the practice tee afterwards," says Steve Williams, talking about his post-game conferences with Tiger Woods. "You might tell the player what you saw earlier that he was doing wrong, how he was swinging it. Or you may just say, 'We had a bit of trouble on this hole' or 'We struggled on this hole, perhaps we should play it this way tomorrow.' Things like that."

The debriefing sessions that caddies go through with their players is the only time they can speak of bad shots or mistakes. During play, everything is oriented towards developing positive vibes and confidence. Caddies are careful on the course to not even use negative language, like "miss," "trouble" or "bad." But once the final putt has dropped, it's OK to discuss or think about the mistakes. As Bobby Jones used to say, he never learned anything from tournaments he won . . . it was the ones he lost that taught him the most about his game and about himself.

So don't dwell on the mistakes, but think about the process that went into making those errant shots and see if there's an adjustment that can be made next time to avoid a similar fate. Remember: the definition of insanity is doing the same thing over and over and expecting different results. If you hit your golf ball into the same lake every time, it's time to try something different!

Compiling statistics that are applicable to your game on your course can go a long way toward developing a winning golf strategy. The secret, as in the rest of the game, is to look at stats as a tool for improvement, not a commentary on your abilities. Berating yourself for being a bad golfer will never contribute to getting the ball into the hole; understanding the why and wherefore will.

Always remember to think like a caddie: positive, upbeat, ready for the next shot, which, as you know by now, is the most important one.

## Important Stats

As noted in the previous chapter, there's a tired old rubric in golf that says one "drives for show, putts for dough." Looking at the PGA Tour for 2009, one can see how true this sentiment is.

Here are the top ten leaders (at the end of October 2009) in the driving distance category:

Robert Garrigus
Bubba Watson
Dustin Johnson
Tad Ridings
Gary Woodland
Nick Watney
J.B. Holmes
Angel Cabrera
Troy Matteson
Harrison Frazer

Compare that list to the top ten money winners:

Tiger Woods
Steve Stricker
Phil Mickelson
Zach Johnson
Kenny Perry
Sean O'Hair
Jim Furyk
Geoff Ogilvy
Lucas Glover
Y.E. Yang

Not a single name on the first list appears on the second! Bashing drives may be fun, but it isn't the best route to winning golf.

Instead, the leading money winners are also leaders in some of the scoring stats, such as *scrambling* (misses the green in regulation but still makes par or better): Woods (1), Stricker (2), Furyk (10); *scoring average*: Woods (1), Stricker (2), Johnson (4), Furyk (8); and *par breakers* (percent of time under par): Woods (1), Stricker (7).

# Chapter 9

## Make Room for Caddie

"Experienced caddies can often tell what kind of game you have after watching two or three swings."

— *James Y. Bartlett*

# 9

# Make Room for Caddie

As Rocco Mediate approached the final green on Sunday of the 2008 U.S. Open at Torrey Pines, he was tied for the lead with Tiger Woods, playing a group behind. As he approached the green, his caddie, Matt Achatz, remembers that Rocco told him, "Make this read, I can't even think!" (Rocco remembers it slightly differently, insisting he said, "Read this putt and make it good!")

Either way, Rocco was certainly glad to have a caddie on his bag whom he could depend on to give him an accurate read on an important putt, at a time of the highest level of pressure and tension imaginable. Would that every golfer facing a pressure shot could turn to someone like that, if not for a good yardage or a good read or a reassuring word, then at least for a bit of comic relief!

In the preceding pages of this book, you have hopefully picked up some worthwhile advice on how to connect with your inner caddie at those important stages in a golf match, and learned how to step back, reassess the situation, think like a caddie thinks, and develop a strong and positive response to the shot facing you. By now you know that even when playing without a caddie, you can still utilize the same kinds of advice, strategy, and help that a real caddie would provide.

Rocco Mediate and Mike Achatz took Tiger and Steve into overtime at the 2008 U.S. Open.

135

But more and more these days, as golf resorts, private country clubs, and even upscale daily-fee facilities are reintroducing caddies, you may get the opportunity to actually play a round with someone carrying your clubs. What then?

First of all, you can still use your new caddie-centric thinking to arrive at your own conclusions about a shot, and match them against your real caddie's conclusions. If both of you agree on a shot, then your confidence level should be extra-high! But in any case, the benefits of having an actual caddie at one's side, in addition to the "mental" caddie recommended in this book, are tremendous.

It's a team thing. The first benefit of playing with a caddie is the sense the golfer gets of having a teammate. While the golfer must still play all the shots, he can rely on his caddie for all the "support" services: information about the next shot, advice on where to aim and the hazards to avoid, and the right message to take you into the shot. A good caddie will provide the following essentials:

- Encouragement after a good shot, understanding after a bad one.

- Conversation and jokes to help the golfer stay loose and relaxed.

- A sense of team support, so important to one's confidence in any competition or match.

When things are going badly, whether it's a series of bad shots or an important missed putt, the caddie is there to remind the golfer that the game isn't over, the next shot awaits, and that good things can still happen. The bad shot can be quickly analyzed ("We missed the break on that putt" or "The wind got that one going sideways") and then forgotten. A caddie will always look for the safe shot back into play after an errant one takes a golfer deep into trouble. And a caddie will always remind the player that it is the *next* shot that is most important, not the last one. That is so invaluable to a golfer who, by himself, might slide into self-pity or even anger after a bad shot. This is the kind of sage advice that is useful to keep in mind whenever you're on a course, whether playing a practice round by yourself or in a competitive tournament with a caddie assisting you.

When things are going well, the caddie is there to keep the confidence level pumped, encourage more good swings, and remind the golfer of the process that produces good results. Playing good golf with a caddie at one's side is like making a shot downhill: it becomes effortless and reinforcing. You will soon find yourself speaking in the possessive voice: "We hit that one well," or "We need a good drive here," or "We read that putt perfectly."

## YOU PLAY — HE CADDIES

Trust your caddie to do his job well. Most golfers are used to gathering their own data before each shot: running around looking for sprinkler heads, studying the scorecard to see where the bunkers and water hazards are, checking the wind, and trying to decide among and between several club choices. In addition, we have to read our own putts, keep track of where an errant shot goes, rake our own bunkers, replace our own divots and ball marks, and wipe our own clubs clean after every shot. When you play with a caddie, you can quit all those mental gymnastics and labor-intensive tasks and simply concentrate on the next shot: where you want it to go and how it's going to get there. When you arrive at your ball, your caddie will have all the information you need: yardages, wind direction, analysis of the lie, a trouble report, and bits of local knowledge. He will have a club recommendation and a swing thought. All you really have to do is relax and make the best swing you can.

## The Donald's Big Bet

Several years ago, Bobby "Rocket" Lytle, the senior caddie at Pebble Beach, hooked up with Donald Trump for the AT&T National Pro-Am. In the round played at Spyglass Hill, they came to the par-3 12th hole. The hole is 178 yards, downhill, and the long, narrow green is protected by a lagoon on the left.

The Donald is a single-digit handicap golfer, and he was thinking 6-iron.

"Take the 5," Rocket urged.

"I think it's a 6," The Donald argued.

"I'm telling you, it's a 5," his caddie insisted.

The debate raged for a few minutes while Trump's pro partner looked on, rolling his eyes.

Finally, Rocket had a brainstorm. "OK, listen," he said. "You just published your book, *The Art of the Deal*. I'll make *you* a deal. Take the 5. If it's the wrong club, you don't have to pay me this week. But if it's right, you pay me double."

Trump thought about that for a bit, and agreed. He always relishes a good bet. He took the 5-iron, made a nice pass at the ball, and everyone watched it fly down the hill towards the green and then go right into the hole for an ace.

At the end of the week, The Donald wrote The Rocket a nice 5-figure check.

## Southern Hospitality at East Lake

During the match, I became aware that I was cheating, or rather my young caddie was doing so for me. Whenever one of my shots strayed into the woods, which bordered the fairways, he would instantly hare off at great speed. On reaching the spot I inevitably found him standing over the ball, which offered both a magnificent lie and an easy recovery line through a most convenient gap in the trees. When this had occurred four or five times I decided something must be done about it, though I was anxious to avoid an embarrassing scene with the caddie who would doubtless deny what was obvious. So I approached my East Lake opponents, told them my fears and heartily apologized. Then one confessed in return: "Don't give it a thought, sir. We had a word with your [caddie] at the start and told him to make sure you enjoyed your game." "But that's cheating," I mildly protested. "No sir," retorted my companion with feeling, "that's Southern hospitality."

— Mark Wilson, in *The Golfer's Bedside Book*

Many modern-day golfers who aren't used to playing with caddies can be hesitant to give up so much "control" over their games, especially to someone they've never met before. Unless you have a bad caddie (and it does happen), this is usually a mistake. Experienced caddies can often tell what kind of game you have after watching two or three swings, which they'll try to do on the practice range. And they frequently know the golf course much better than you do. So if your caddie tells you that, for instance, a 150-yard shot calls for an easy 6, and you try to insist that you always hit your 7-iron 150 yards, you'd do well to listen. He might know things you don't: for instance, that the hole plays a little uphill, or that clearing that front bunker is important, or that being slightly long is much better than being slightly short.

It can also be amazingly relaxing and surprisingly stress-reducing to arrive at your ball after a walk up the fairway, be handed a club and told how hard or easy to hit it, and be given something to aim at and encouraged to let 'er rip. Instead of worrying about all the information that went into that decision, golf becomes a much easier game when one can step up to the ball and obey someone else's instructions. Allow yourself to be coached by your caddie and trust his advice. The results will often be remarkable.

Another Nicklaus father-son team: Jack with Jackie on the bag.

## THE TOP 5 THINGS THAT MOST CADDIES HATE

We surveyed several dozen caddies to find out what golfers could do to make the caddie's job easier and more enjoyable. Here's their list:

### 1. Heavy golf bags

Do you have a Burton Tour-size leather bag? Caddies hate to see those come out of the trunk of a car! If you're planning to play a round with a caddie, do the poor fellow a favor and bring a smaller, lighter golf bag.

Also, eliminate as much weight as you can. Most of us are packrats when it comes to golf balls, stuffing as many sleeves as we can into the various compartments and never, ever, throwing away old, scuffed balls. Experienced caddies will go straight for the ball compartment and start pulling out all the worn, dirty balls, and any new ones over about a dozen. Getting rid of the unnecessary weight of old balls will be appreciated by your caddie.

Likewise, go through the other compartments in your golf bag and remove all the other items you won't need that day: the extra pair of shoes, rain gear, sweaters, or wind jackets, bottles of water, your ten-year collection of divot tools and golf tees, and anything else that weighs over an ounce! Of course, if the forecast is for rain, keep the rain gear handy. And remember, you're likely to need such gear if you're playing anywhere in Great Britain or Ireland, where even a cloudless blue-sky day on the first tee is no guarantee you won't get caught in a rain shower by the 9th green.

Make sure you have just fourteen clubs: the day you play with a caddie is not the day to try out three new drivers and four new sand wedges. You can also remove the ball retriever. Your caddie will be the first to tell you: "Let it go . . . they make more golf balls every day!"

### 2. Golf bags not designed for walking

Caddies love the modern "walking" bags with double backpacker straps and stand-up legs. Caddies hate old golf bags with uncomfortable shoulder straps (or no straps at all!).

### 3. Gimmicky stuff

Caddies hate things that slow them down. Golf bags with individual holes for each golf club, instead of open-padded sections, are a pain. So are head covers on irons. Caddies can usually manage to keep track of the head covers for your driver and 3-wood (don't be surprised to see them tucked away for the round — pulling them on and off after every use takes time), but if they have to worry about iron covers too, they won't be happy.

### 4. Golfers who don't respect the game

Your caddie will put up with almost anything. After all, he's being paid for his time. But caddies appreciate golfers who demonstrate their respect for the game by following proper etiquette and demeanor.

Wear the proper golf attire and make sure you are neat.

Be respectful of other players and caddies.

Turn off the cell phone and other electronic gadgets. They irritate other players and the caddies as well. If you can't stand to be unconnected for four hours, then stay in the office.

### 5. Golfers who don't remember the Golden Rule

Treat your caddie as you would wish to be treated. Learn his name and use it. Treat him with respect. Thank him for good advice. A caddie who feels part of the competitive experience, who is treated with courtesy and respect for his knowledge and professionalism, will respond with better effort, and that, in turn, will result in a better round of golf for both of you.

# Chapter 10
## The Caddie Hall of Fame

"Success is not measured by what a person accomplishes,
but by the opposition that person has encountered,
and the courage he or she possesses to complete
the mission while helping kids along the way."

— Dennis Cone,
founder and CEO, World Caddie Headquarters
of the Professional Caddies Association

Caddie Hall of Fame inductees: (left to right) Sam "Killer" Foy (caddie for Hale Irwin), Angelo Argea (caddie for Jack Nicklaus), Jim Clark (a centenarian and longtime looper at Baltusrol), and Alfred "Rabbit" Dyer (caddie for Gary Player) with PCA co-founder Laura Cone.

# 10

## The Caddie Hall of Fame

Although he didn't know it, when Jeff "Squeaky" Medlin died tragically in 1997 of leukemia, he helped foster the founding of the Professional Caddies Association and Foundation.

Like almost all caddies on the professional tours, Medlin had little in the way of savings, retirement, or medical benefits, despite his years of successful service to the likes of Nick Price, John Daly, and other PGA Tour winners. Recognizing the need to provide caddies with a stronger financial base, a former part-time caddie named Dennis Cone decided to do something.

Cone had already started working with the Junior Golf Association of Central Florida as their president and later cofounded with PGA Tour player Donnie Hammond the Evergreen Youth Foundation, which is now known as The Caddie Foundation. Initial funding was received from the Marriott Vacation Club, caddie Mike "Fluff" Cowan, and others to launch the Professional Caddies Association (PCA) Worldwide to provide members, caddies, their families, and supporters with additional income opportunities and access to medical and retirement benefits.

In addition, the PCA's mission includes providing caddie services and certification thorough educational and communication programs worldwide. To date, the PCA has helped certify and train more than 10,000 caddies through its educational and training programs. As golf has returned to its roots as a walking game, the PCA has been in the forefront of recruiting and training a new generation of caddies.

Working with the PGA Credit Union and the Greco Planning Group, the PCA administers the PCA Caddie Benevolent and Retirement Fund to provide financial benefits to retired caddie members.

Working with golf and country clubs worldwide, the PCA has been in the forefront of new caddie programs, with initiatives such as the PCA Eagle Guide FORE Caddie programs, which include training in CPR and defibrillator applications. With the recent addition of caddie services offered at the home courses of the PGA of America, the PGA Tour, and many five-star resorts worldwide, there is good evidence that caddie programs are on the rise again.

In 1999, the PCA inducted the first class into the Caddie Hall of Fame to recognize the important service that caddies have provided both to professional and recreational golfers over the years. Honorees include both active and retired caddies, longtime caddie masters at some of the world's foremost country clubs

and golf resorts, and others who have supported caddies and caddie programs. The Caddie Hall of Fame, which eventually will be located in St. Augustine, Florida, is looking to open botanical tree gardens at major golf courses and computer-based information centers worldwide, which would be housed in replicas of the old starter house from St. Andrews, Scotland. As founder/CEO of the World Caddie Headquarters of the PCA, Dennis Cone's philosophy is: "Success is not measured by what a person accomplishes, but by the opposition that person has encountered, and the courage he or she possesses to complete the mission while helping kids along the way."

Professional Caddies Association founder and president Dennis Cone with his wife Laura.

# The Caddie Hall of Fame

Inductees into the Hall of Fame include:

### Class of 1999

- **Lynda Barco** (namesake of the Lynda Barco Spirit Award, honoring individuals and corporate supporters of PCA Worldwide)

- **Francis Ouimet** (former caddie, 1913 US Open champion, and namesake of the Francis Ouimet Scholarship Fund for caddies)

- **Charles "Chick" Evans** (former caddie, U.S. Open champion in 1920 and founder of the Chick Evans Scholarship Fund for caddies)

- **Eddie Lowery** (Francis Ouimet's 10-year-old caddie in 1913)

- **Jeff "Squeaky" Medlin** (caddie for Nick Price and John Daly)

- **Alfie Fyles** (caddie for Tom Watson's five British Open wins)

- **Angelo Argea** (longtime caddie for Jack Nicklaus)

- **Herman Mitchell** (longtime caddie for Lee Trevino)

- **Peter Coleman** (caddie for Bernhard Langer)

- **Mike "Fluff" Cowan** (caddie for Peter Jacobsen, Tiger Woods, Jim Furyk)

- **Adolphus "Golf Ball" Hull** (caddie for Raymond Floyd, Lee Elder, Calvin Peete)

- **Emil "Smitty" Smith** (caddie for Bob Charles, Ben Crenshaw)

- **Henry "Gado" Rice** (caddie for George Knudson)

- **Donnie "Wad" Wanstall** (caddie for Mark O'Meara, Curtis Strange)

- **Carl Jackson** (caddie for Ben Crenshaw's two Masters wins)

- **Ralph Coffey** (caddie for Deane Beman, George Burns)

- **Tony Battistello** (caddie manager for 41 years at Sunset Ridge Country Club)

PCA Caddie Hall of Famer Alfred 'Rabbit' Dyer with Gary Player of South Africa during the USPGA Championship at Shoal Creek in Birmingham, Alabama in August 1984.

# ★ The Caddie Hall of Fame ★

## Class of 2000

- **Lorne "Rabbit" LeBere** (30-year PGA Tour caddie)

- **Sam "Killer" Foy** (caddie for Hale Irwin)

- **Ross "Cotton" Young** (caddie for 65 years at Saucon Valley Country Club)

- **Ernest "Creamy" Carolon** (caddie for Arnold Palmer)

- **Alfred "Rabbit" Dyer** (caddie for Gary Player)

- **James "Tip" Anderson** (Arnold Palmer's caddie at St. Andrews, Scotland)

- **Greg Rita** (caddie for Curtis Strange, John Daly, Mark O'Meara, David Duval)

- **Willie Peterson** (Jack Nicklaus's caddie at Augusta National Golf Club, GA)

- **Roscoe Jones** (caddie for Nancy Lopez)

- **Lee Lynch** (caddie for Al Geiberger)

- **Jim Clark** (longtime caddie at Baltusrol Golf Club, NJ)

- **Willie Aitchison** (caddie master at British Open)

- **Freddie Bennett** (longtime caddie master at Augusta National Golf Club, GA)

- **Steve Burks** (Marriott Vacation Club, recipient of the Lynda Barco Spirit Award)

# The Caddie Hall of Fame

## Class of 2001

- **John "Irish" O'Reilly** (European tour caddie and author)

- **Jerry "Dee" Darden** (caddie for Beth Daniel)

- **Patrick J. Collins** (caddie master at Winged Foot Golf Club, NY)

- **Gary Chapman** (country singer who recorded "Five Feet Away" for the PCA and was the recipient of the Lynda Barco Spirit Award)

## Class of 2002

- **Pete McCann** (caddie for 45 years at Alpine Country Club, NJ)

- **Carl S. Laib** (caddie for Patty Sheehan)

- **Leonard Ciccone** (longtime caddie master, Montclair Country Club, NJ)

- **Sam Johnson** (caddie in Philadelphia section of PGA for 50 years)

- **Scott Hudson** ("Golf Nut of the Year")

- **Pedro Eulalio Lopez Gonzales** (70 years of service at Tijuana Country Club, Mexico)

- **Martin Roy** (caddie master, Carnoustie Golf Links, Scotland)

- **Mike Granuzzo** (founder, Caddie Master Enterprises, recipient of the Lynda Barco Spirit Award)

Leonard Ciccone was honored by the PCA Caddie Hall of Fame for his 65 years of service, including his stint as the caddie for Yogi Berra in 1988.

Nick Faldo won several major championships with Swedish caddie Fanny Sunesson on the bag.

# The Caddie Hall of Fame

## Class of 2003

**Bruce Edwards** (longtime caddie for Tom Watson)

**Fanny Sunesson** (caddie for Nick Faldo)

**Terry McNamara** (caddie for Annika Sorenstam)

**Willie McRae** (longtime caddie at Pinehurst Country Club, NC)

**James Pernice** (longtime caddie at Oakmont Country Club, PA, and caddie for Sam Snead and Bobby Jones)

**Saverio "Mac" Macaluso** (longtime caddie at Oakmont Country Club, PA)

**Jerry "Woody" Woodward** (longtime LPGA caddie)

**Charlie Winton** (longtime caddie at Gleneagles Golf Club, Scotland)

**Andrew Butley "The Rooney"** (longtime caddie and teacher at Tramore Golf Club, Ireland)

**Andrew Dickson** (first named caddie in history and club maker)

**Don Bobillo** (volunteer caddie master, Phoenix Open, AZ)

**Dennis M. Dowd** (Hitachi America, recipient of the Lynda Barco Spirit Award)

## Class of 2004

**Van Costa** (longtime PGA and LPGA caddie)

**Oscar Goings** (longtime caddie master, Winchester Golf Club, MA)

**David Vincent Williams and Mike Geiger** (songwriters, "Five Feet Away," and recipients of the Lynda Barco Spirit Award)

# The Caddie Hall of Fame

## Class of 2005

- **Arthur "Bucky" Walters** (father and caddie of trick-shot artist Dennis Walters)

- **Dr. Michael Cohen** (vascular surgeon and golfer, recipient of the Lynda Barco Spirit Award))

- **William J. Survilla** (longtime caddie master at Oak Park Country Club, IL)

- **"Old" Tom Morris** (longtime keeper of the links at St. Andrews and British Open champion)

- **Gene Sarazen** (caddie and golf champion)

- **Willie Park, Sr.** (former caddie and three-time British Open champion)

## Class of 2006

- **Bradley S. Klein Ph.D.** (former caddie, architecture editor for *Golfweek*)

- **Roger Martinez** (caddie for Gene Sarazen, Ben Hogan, Jack Nicklaus)

- **Walter "Cricket" Pritchett** (caddie for Masters winner Charles Coody)

- **Willie "Pappy" Stokes** ('grandfather of caddies' at Augusta National, caddied for four different Masters champions)

- **Gerry W. Barousse, Jr.** (longtime caddie for U.S. Blind Golf Association champion Pat Browne)

- **Kevin J. Sullivan** (longtime caddie for blind golfer Bill McMahon)

- **Douglas Ellsworth** (caddie manager and director of the Sankaty Head caddie camp, Nantucket, MA)

- **J. Michael "Mike" Hartman** (PCA founding treasurer, recipient of the Lynda Barco Spirit Award)

## Old Tom and the "Ragged Cads"

A true son of St. Andrews, born June 16, 1821, on North Street just a block or two from the first tee of the Old Course, Tom Morris started hitting golf balls almost as soon as he could walk. His father was a mailman, but at a young age Tom began to learn the craft of making golf balls, the "featheries" of the time, and later worked as apprentice under the watchful eye of Allan Robertson, the keeper of the links.

It is not known if Tom — today known as "Old Tom Morris" to distinguish him from his son, Young Tom, also a champion golfer — ever caddied at St. Andrews. As a ball and club maker and later as the keeper of the links, or head professional, it is likely that he didn't. Caddies in his day tended to be young boys or older men without any other employable skills.

But as Old Tom's fame as a competitor began to rise, he certainly knew the best caddies at St. Andrews, as well as at Leith and Musselburgh, the other two main courses of his era. Later, after a dispute with Robertson, Old Tom moved to Prestwick to take over the links there. It was due largely to his fame and reputation that the first twelve Open Championships were played at Old Prestwick.

Old Tom won four of those Opens; his son won another four before dying at the young age of 24. Both the Morrises also played challenge matches against the other Scottish professionals of their era which captured the attention of the country in which almost everyone, rich and poor, man or woman, played the game.

The following is the beginning of a narrative poem, author unknown, which describes the 1st hole of one such match in 1866 at St. Andrews, with Old Tom and his partner, Colonel Walker, going against two men of St. Andrews: D.L. Burn and David Lamb.

*Attended by their ragged cads,*

*Four dirty young St. Andrews lads,*

*Waiting each player's stern command*

*To tee his ball with practised hand.*

*Burn struck his ball towards the burn,*

*The Colonel followed in his turn,*

*The first lay sweetly on the sward,*

*The second met its just reward,*

*And plunged into the muddy stream.*

*Not a good stroke was that, I ween,*

*Which left poor Tom to play one more,*

*Whilst Lamb and Burn holed out in four.*

Old Tom Morris, Keeper of the Links.

# The Caddie Hall of Fame

## Class of 2007

- **William "Bill" Thomas** (caddie for 69 years at Wee Burn Country Club, CT)

- **Carl "Uncle Carl" Eisenbrei** (longtime caddie at Congress Lake Club, OH)

- **Jackie and Percy Hall** (parents of deaf golfer Kevin Hall)

- **Frank Selva** (longtime caddie manager and PGA head pro at Race Brook Country Club, CT)

- **Rick Schad** (graphic artist, recipient of the Lynda Barco Spirit Award)

- **Lance Barrow** (CBS Sports producer and recipient of the Gene Sarazen Spirit Award)

## Class of 2008

- **Elijah Brown** (longtime caddie at Seminole Golf Club, FL)

- **Tom Gorman** (longtime caddie manager, Beverly Country Club, MA)

- **Charlie DeLucca** (leading figure in south Florida golf)

- **Max Elbin** (former president of PGA of America and head pro at Burning Tree Club, Washington, DC, recipient of the Gene Sarazen Spirit Award)

- **Dr. John Reynolds** (Club Car vice president, recipient of the Gene Sarazen Spirit Award)

- **James V. Burgess Jr.** (former caddie and lawyer, recipient of the Gene Sarazen Spirit Award)

- **Jack Lucas** (former caddie, recipient of the Lynda Barco Spirit Award)

When the last putt drops, the winning team — caddie and player — can celebrate.

# Acknowledgments

When Dennis Cone, who founded and heads the Professional Caddies Association Worldwide, decided he wanted to create a book that would mine the prodigious and accumulated knowledge of his band of brothers — the caddies in the PCA's Hall of Fame as well as those working full-time both on the various professional tours and at country clubs and resorts across the country and around the world — he naturally turned to *our* band of brothers: the fraternity of golf writers in the Golf Writers Association of America.

Somehow along the way I got volun-nominated to take charge of the project, which you are now holding in your hands. Moreso with most projects, however, this one truly represents a collective effort by many people.

At the top of the list is Dennis Cone himself. A force of nature, Dennis is an entrepreneur, a true believer, a tireless cheerleader, and someone who knows everyone in the golf world. He dragged us through the planning process, wrangled up a publisher, and cheered us on as we struggled with a ridiculously tight deadline. This may not be exactly the book he had in mind, but it's exactly the book that he made happen out of thin air.

Next come the writers who participated in the project by interviewing caddies and writing, editing, and rewriting various portions of the text. My thanks for the contributions from this highly talented group: Dave Gould, Mark Nelson, and Reid Champagne researched, interviewed, and wrote; Anderson Craigg, a caddie himself, contributed to several chapters. Two other members of the team, John Coyne and Rick Woelfel, had prior commitments during the writing part of the project, but their early contributions were invaluable. A special thanks goes to Daniel Weigand and Vicki Aitken, who kindly allowed us to use excerpts from the caddie interviews they did in their book, *Caddy-Talk: Psychology of Being a Great Caddy* (2007, Dawvija Publishing, Milton Keynes, UK). You can get more information about their book at www.caddy-talk.com and about sports psychology and golf performance in general at www.AchieveAcumen.com.

Our appreciation goes to our agent, Marilyn Allen of the firm Allen O'Shea Literary Agency, who helped us split a few hairs, if not infinitives, during contract negotiations; and Mark Chimsky-Lustig, our editor at Sellers Publishing, who somehow turned the mad rush of words into a coherent whole. Plaudits to the rest of the Sellers team as well: Ronnie Sellers, Robin Haywood, Mary Baldwin, and Charlotte Smith.

Special thanks to my beautiful wife Susan who s'cused me while I disappear'd into my computer for a few weeks to slay this wretched beast, for her unflagging support, insightful editing, and quiet understanding.

Finally, a heartfelt thanks goes to caddies . . . those who graciously responded to our questions and all those who have ever carried someone's bag. Unique in all of sports, these non-playing partners in the game provide an invaluable service to their players, whether in a major tournament or a weekend Nassau at the club. They carry for us, and sometimes they carry us. But they have the vantage of a front-row seat and they can teach us a lot about ourselves, and the great game of golf.

All you have to do is listen.

*— James Y. Bartlett*


First, I want to thank God, my mom, and my wonderful wife, Laura, for all the love and guidance, inspiration and support they've shown during my twenty-year quest to honor the great stewards of the game, the caddies.

Thanks to the many other friends and family who took time out of their busy schedules to help with this ongoing mission. My gratitude to Mike Hartman and the PCA Board of Trustees for overseeing the mission of the Professional Caddies Association ( PCA ) and the PCA Foundation, and to Grammy winner Michael Bolton, who recorded the song "Five Feet Away" to benefit the PCA and all charities worldwide. Thanks also to the golf writers at GWAA, UK, Worldwide and my mentor, Jim Walters, who taught me to speak from the heart. And to Straton Wilhelm for your heart.

Joe Louis Barrow Jr., Steve Mona, and PGA Tour player Donnie Hammond, as well as the PGA of America, the PGA Tour, and the LPGA have all been wonderful supporters of the PCA over the years, as has the Francis Ouimet Foundation, the Western Golf Association, and many other caddie associations around the world that have helped with education and caddie training programs. Caddie on.

A special thank you to golf greats Arnold Palmer and Ben Crenshaw for generously contributing the Foreword and Preface to this book.

Our work is ongoing as we continue to honor and celebrate great caddies of the past and present and help train a new generation of caddies for the future. I invite you to join with us in this work to help make our game even greater in the years ahead.

To my grandkids, who light up my life. To all the kids I have seen around the world carrying that big bag with a smile — you get my heart pumping to continue the mission to help the kids and the game. At the end of the day, "It's all about the kids." Please join the mission - visit www.PCAhq.com.

*— Dennis Cone*

# About the Authors

**JAMES Y. BARTLETT** is the overall project editor and main writer for *Think Like a Caddie, Play Like a Pro*. A longtime golf writer and editor, Bartlett has also published four golf mystery novels (The Hacker series, Yeoman House Books) and three books of golf nonfiction. He is a former features editor at *Golfweek*, was editor of *Luxury Golf* magazine, and executive editor of *Caribbean Travel & Life* magazine. He was the golf columnist for *Forbes FYI* magazine for twelve years, during which time he wrote about his caddie experiences with Jack Nicklaus and Arnold Palmer. He is a fulltime freelance writer and editor now living in Rhode Island.

**DENNIS** and **LAURA CONE** are co-writers/publishers and co-founders of the Professional Caddies Association (PCA), The Caddie Association (TCA) and The Caddie Foundation (TCF). Dennis is a seventh-generation Floridian, who left the business world in 1982 to serve as president of the nonprofit Junior Golf Association of Central Florida until 1990, an organization that has helped thousands of kids get into the  game of golf, and also helped send at least four players to the PGA Tour, including Chris DeMarco. Laura was the former financial consultant at the World Trade Center and past president of the PCA. Since 1997, the PCA has helped train and certify more than 10,000 new caddies around the world and its PCA caddie manual has been used at more than fifty top country clubs. The PCA also sponsors the PCA Caddie Hall of Fame (www.PCAFhq.org) to honor noted caddies from past and present. They ask readers to join the Friends of PCA today!

**DAVID GOULD** is an editor, book author, and journalist with twenty-plus years of professional experience. He has specialized in golf, travel, and related lifestyle topics as a magazine editor with *Links* (chief editor, 2000-2005), *Golf Illustrated* (executive editor, 1989-91) and *Golf Shop Operations* (chief editor 1986-89). Currently, he serves as editor-at-large for *Travel + Leisure Golf*, an American Express title. He has published four books, including *The Golfer's Code* (Fairchild, 1994) and *Q School Confidential: Inside Golf's Cruelest Tournament* (St. Martins, 1999). He has worked on several book projects as a manuscript editor, including a lengthy collaboration with Jim McLean on McLean's minor classic *The Eight-Step Swing*. Gould is a 1980 graduate of Wesleyan University in Middletown, CT, where he was a Francis Ouimet Scholar. He is married to the novelist Rachel Basch.

**MARK NELSON** is a public relations consultant and former political journalist who regularly writes about golf both as a regular contributor to *GolfStyles Washington* and on his popular blog, "Mr. Fairway," (http://mrfairway.blogspot.com). Nelson, a member of the Golf Writers Association of America, also wrote the lead article on business golf for a special online and insert edition of *Business Week* and *Golf Digest* and last year he authored a feature on aspiring club professionals that appeared in *Washingtonian*. His non-golf work has been published in a variety of magazines, including *D Magazine*, *Houston City*, and *Regardies*. In 1984 he co-authored *The Semi-Official Dallas Cowboys Hater's Handbook*, published by Collier Books of Macmillan Publishing. Nelson previously was a reporter for *The Associated Press*, the *Fort Worth Star-Telegram*, and *The Dallas Morning News*.

**REID CHAMPAGNE** is currently a regular contributor for *Delaware Today* magazine. A writer for more than twenty-five years, Champagne began writing about golf ten years ago. He is the contributing editor for *Today Media's* annual Golf Guide, published throughout Delaware and southeastern Pennsylvania. His work has appeared nationally in *Golf*, *Golfweek*, and *Links* magazines. His golf fiction has appeared in the former *Florida Golf Journal*. His essay, "When You Wish Upon a Par," appeared in the 2002 collection, *Chicken Soup for the Golfer's Soul: The Second Round*. Married and the father of three, Champagne, along with his forbearing wife of thirty-four years, recently became an empty nester, which surprisingly has not led to the dramatic increase in time to play golf he had always imagined it would.

**ANDERSON CRAIGG** is a native of Barbados, where he began a career as a caddie as a young "ball shagger" at the Sandy Lane resort. After a ten-year career on the Royal Barbados Police Force, he emigrated to the United States to continue his education in business administration, yet continued as a caddie at Deepdale and Sebonak clubs on Long Island, and The Bears Club in Jupiter, Florida. He has published a book, *Professional Golf Caddie Secrets Exposed*, a comprehensive home study guide that is based on a learn-by-doing method.

# Photo Credits:

Cover Image © Donald Miralle/Getty Images Sport; p. 5 © Steven Dinberg; p. 6 © Marc Feldman/Getty Images Sport; p. 8 © Andrew Redington/Getty Images Sport; p. 10 © Steven Dinberg; p. 15 © Steven Dinberg; p. 16 © PCA Library/Dennis Cone with permission; p. 18 © Jeff Haynes/AFP/Getty Images Sport; p. 21 © Francis Ouimet Scholarship Foundation; p. 22 © Andrew Redington/Getty Images Sport; p. 26 © Steven Dinberg; p. 29 © PCA Library/Dennis Cone with permission; p. 30 © Heniz Kluetmeier/Sports Illustrated/Getty Images Sport; p. 32 © Brian Spurlock; p. 34 © Brian Spurlock; p. 37 © Bob Thomas/Bob Thomas Sports Photography/Getty Images Sport; p. 41 © Brian Spurlock; p. 42 © Steven Dinberg; p. 44 © Steven Dinberg; p. 46 © Steven Dinberg; p. 47 © Brian Spurlock; p. 50 © Steven Dinberg; p. 54 © Dennis Cone with AGJ Golf Library permission; p. 58 © Steven Dinberg; p. 60 © Brian Spurlock; p. 62 © Robert Beck/Sports Illustrated/Getty Images Sport; p. 64 © Darren Carroll/Getty Images Sport; p. 65 © Jeff Gross/Getty Images Sport; p. 67 © Steven Dinberg; p. 68 © Steven Dinberg; p. 71 © Robert Beck/Sports Illustrated/Getty Images Sport; p. 72 © Steven Dinberg; p. 74 © Steven Dinberg; p. 76 © PCA Library/Dennis Cone with permission; p. 80 © Andrew Redington/Getty Images Sport; p. 83 © PCA Library/Dennis Cone with permission; p. 84 © Steven Dinberg; P. 86 © Brian Spurlock; p. 91 © Steven Dinberg; p. 92 © Andrew Redington/Getty Images Sport; p. 93 © Historic Golf Photos – The Ron Watts Collection © 1998 - 2009; p. 95 © Steven Dinberg; p. 96 © Al Tielemans/Sports Illustrated/Getty Images Sport; p. 97 © Steven Dinberg; p. 105 © Brian Spurlock; p. 106 © Stan Badz/US PGA Tour/Getty Images Sport; p. 108 © Tannen Maury/AFP/Getty Images Sport; p. 110 © Dennis Cone with AGJ Golf Library permission; p. 112 © Stan Badz/US PGA Tour/Getty Images Sport; p. 113 © Brian Spurlock; p. 114 © Brian Spurlock; p. 117 © Steven Dinberg; p. 119 © Brian Spurlock; p. 120 © George Crocker Professional photography www.g-pik.co.uk; p. 122 © Steven Dinberg; p. 124 © George Crocker Professional photography www.g-pik.co.uk; p. 126 © Steven Dinberg; p. 128 © Harry How/Getty Images Sport; p. 132 © Steven Dinberg; p. 134 © Robert Beck/Sports Illustrated/Getty Images Sport; p. 139 © Steven Dinberg; p. 142 © Historic Golf Photos – The Ron Watts Collection © 1998 - 2009; p. 144 © PCA Library/Dennis Cone with permission; p. 146 © PCA Library/Dennis Cone with permission; p. 148 © David Cannon/Getty Images Sport; p. 151 © PCA Library/Dennis Cone with permission; p. 152 © Bob Thomas/Bob Thomas Sports Photography/Getty Images Sport; p. 155 © Historic Golf Photos – The Ron Watts Collection © 1998 - 2009; p. 157 © Steven Dinberg.

The source for quotes on pages 33, 35, and back cover (Steve Williams); 36 (Mike Patterson); 38 (Steve Williams); 97-98 (Steve Williams) is *Caddy-Talk: Psychology of Being a Great Caddy* by Vicki Aitken and Daniel A. Weigand (Dawvija Publishing, 2007) reprinted with the authors' permission.